P9-CPV-599

Progression Blackjack

PROGRESSION BLACKJACK

Exposing the Card Counting Myth

Donald A. Dahl

A Citadel Press Book
Published by Carol Publishing Group

Carol Publishing Group Edition, 1998

Copyright © 1993 by Donald A. Dahl
All rights reserved. No part of this book may be reproduced in any form,
except by a newspaper or magazine reviewer who wishes to quote brief
passages in connection with a review.

A Citadel Press Book
Published by Carol Publishing Group
Citadel Press is a registered trademark of Carol Communications, Inc.

Editorial, sales and distribution, rights and permissions inquiries
should be addressed to Carol Publishing Group, 120 Enterprise Avenue,
Secaucus, N.J. 07094

In Canada: Canadian Manda Group, One Atlantic Avenue, Suite 105,
Toronto, Ontario M6K 3E7

Carol Publishing Group books may be purchased in bulk at special
discounts for sales promotions, fund-raising, or educational purposes.
Special editions can be created to specifications. For details, contact
Special Sales Department, Carol Publishing Group, 120 Enterprise Avenue,
Secaucus, N.J. 07094

Manufactured in the United States of America
10 9 8 7 6 5 4

Library of Congres Cataloging-in-Publication Data

Dahl, Donald A.
Progression blackjack: exposing the card counting myth /
by Donald A. Dahl.
p. cm.
"A Citadel Press book."
ISBN 0-8065-1396-9
1. Blackjack (Game). I Title.
GV1295.B55D34 1993
795.4′2—dc20   92-38085
                                                          CIP

Knowing that billions of hard-earned dollars have been lost by millions of well-motivated but misinformed and underfinanced card counters, my own motivation to write *Progression Blackjack* became well grounded. The love, help, and, most of all, encouragement given by my father, Warner ("Buzz") Dahl, and my wife, Robin, made it all possible.

Contents

Preface

The game of blackjack/twenty-one should be simple, exciting, fun, and, most of all, profitable! The easy-to-understand approach to the game taught in this book makes it possible to beat the casinos under today's rules and multiple-deck games. One should not have to be a mathematical wizard with a large bankroll in order to beat the game of blackjack. The typical casino patron does not have the thousands of dollars required to support the "card counting" systems promoted by so-called experts. Nor should a player be required to risk such sums in a game of chance.

With the betting progressions, winning play strategy and money management discussed in this book, you will enjoy the game as never before. You will learn to be a serious threat to the casino's profits by risking a minimal amount of your own money with a good chance of taking large profits from the "house." Given today's rules, shuffle criteria, multiple-deck shoes and table limits, casino owners do not fear "card counters," "double up-betters" and so-called high rollers." They do, however, shudder at the thought of a player who consistently bets the minimum while losing and makes large bets while winning. Wouldn't you?

Numerous books have been written on the subject, the most famous being *Beat the Dealer* by Dr. Edward O. Thorp, a professor of mathematics at the University of California. Almost every book published since has been based on Dr. Thorp's card counting strategy, with only minor changes. The problem is, these books are based on the blackjack rules and practices of the 1960s! Dr. Thorp's book was a powerful and serious threat to the casinos. Allowed to case entire decks of cards, "counters" were able to bet large sums of money with minimal risk simply by discerning the values of the remaining cards. To add to their advantage, extremely liberal rules were in effect. Players were allowed to double-down on any two cards, split aces repeatedly, and take more than one card on a split ace! Under such conditions it is quite obvious that *Beat the Dealer* was a must for knowledgeable blackjack players.

The casinos were literally forced by Dr. Thorp to change the rules of blackjack drastically. Card counters have lost the advantage through rule changes and the use of multiple-deck shoes. A player is now lucky to see merely two-thirds to three-quarters of the decks before the dealer reshuffles. Single- and double-deck games are rare throughout the world today. Some casinos in Nevada advertise single-deck games to lure card counters, but then dealers shuffle as often as necessary to thwart a player advantage.

Contrary to the beliefs of experts, card counting is not necessary to win money. In fact, this book discusses why card counting can be more of a deterrent. Not only is card counting overrated, it is not fun! Card counting requires a great deal of concentration and hard work. A card counter must keep track of all cards played (the easy part), and continuously divide the "count" by the number of remaining cards. This information is used to determine bets and deviation from basic play strategy. The end result of counting strategy is to give the player a slight advantage over the house.

My system requires little concentration, takes maximum advantage of favorable cards, enables large bets to be made on a small budget, and puts the fun back into the game. Read on!

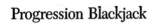

Progression Blackjack

1

Casino Blackjack

Walking into a gambling casino is the adult equivalent to a child entering Disneyland for the first time. It is a completely different world. The excitement in the air is amplified by the sounds of money gushing from slots, with bells and sirens screaming. Spirited cheers and moans from excited players can often be heard at the numerous blackjack and craps tables.

Never forget that the casino is a large business establishment with the goal of removing money from your wallet. On a day-to-day-basis, casinos never lose. The odds on all their games are in the house's favor. Without such an advantage, the casinos would not be in the gambling business.

Today's casinos are, as a whole, completely honest. They have too much to lose if caught cheating. Most of their profits come from the small bettor who arrives expecting to lose. These players, only too often, make the casino's goal easy by throwing money on the tables with little knowledge of the game they are playing.

Of the games offered, craps and blackjack give the player the best odds of winning. In craps, the odds are fixed and never vary. In other words, the chance of rolling a 7 will always be 16.7 percent (6/36), regardless of the number of 7's previously thrown. In blackjack, however, the house percentage varies as cards are depleted. On many occasions, the odds can actually shift in favor of the player! This is what makes blackjack the best game in the house. By taking advantage of favorable situations through increased betting and proper play, the game can be beaten!

To attract customers, the casinos in Nevada offer numerous benefits and outstanding deals. They provide excellent meals dirt cheap and top-name entertainment at relatively low prices. The cost of rooms in the plushest of casinos is often below that of equivalent rooms in your hometown. Many casinos offer packages that include lodging, airfare, cash rebates, shows, and other inducements. These deals can't be beat! The only requirement is that the customer spend a certain amount of time at the gaming tables to receive all of the benefits. Most casinos also offer free drinks to bettors while they are playing.

Atlantic City, on the other hand, has relatively fewer casinos and is the only city with casino gambling on the East Coast (as of this writing). The casinos have an obvious East Coast monopoly and apparently feel they do not need to lure customers. Food and lodging are outrageously priced. If you are staying more than a few days, it is less expensive in the long run to purchase a "gambling package" to Nevada, even if you live on the East Coast! Needless to say, if you live close to Atlantic City, by all means go there to gamble, but consider eating meals in the local restaurants. I had my first $7 hamburger in an Atlantic City casino!

Blackjack is played the same in all casinos. The number of decks used, and some specific rules, may vary. Atlantic City casinos all play by the same rules and deal multiple decks out of a shoe; they are not allowed to vary from state controlled rules. In Nevada, the rules are generally the same, although each casino may vary the rules and number of decks used. Single-deck games are available and casinos with more liberal rules in favor of the player can be found.

For the present, I will discuss the procedures and rules followed by the majority of the casinos throughout the world. The blackjack game consists of a semicircular table laid out to accommodate up to seven players. Each position or "spot" is provided with a stool upon which a player may sit. The dealer stands on the opposite side of the table and deals from a "shoe" holding up to eight decks of cards.

When a table is first opened up for play, the cards are spread out, face up, on the table. Once a player sits down, the dealer begins to shuffle the cards. After the cards are shuffled, the dealer presents a colored plastic card to one of the players which is used to "cut" the decks. After the cut, the dealer inserts the plastic card somewhere near the last two-thirds to three-quarters of all the cards. The cut made by the player determines the first card dealt from the shoe; the cut made by the dealer determines when the play from that shoe is to be concluded. All of the cards are then placed in the shoe.

The first card from the shoe is "burned" by placing it in the discard pile. All players are expected to place their bets prior to the dealing out of the card. Minimum and maximum bets allowed are posted at the table. The minimum is usually $5, $10, or $25. The maximum varies from $100 to $1,000. A player must be careful to ensure that he or she is at a table with the desired limits. Tables with minimums of less than $5 can be found in Nevada but are unheard of in Atlantic City, on cruise ships, and in the Bahamas. Bets are placed on the designated spots in front of the players. After all bets are made, the first hand is dealt.

Each player is betting that he or she will reach a total card value of 21, or as close as possible, without exceeding 21, and have a higher total value than the dealer. The player is only competing with the house, represented by the dealer. The dealer is attempting to beat all players at the table and must follow specific rules regarding when to "hit" or "stay." The cards are dealt to each player starting at the dealer's left. Each player receives one card up, including the dealer. Each player then receives a second card up. The dealer places his or her second card face down, the value of which is not known to the players. Starting with the first player to the dealer's left, each must either receive another card (hit); keep what they have (stay); split (if two cards are of the same value); or double-down (if the two-card value equals 10 or 11). The actions taken are based on the player's own cards with knowledge of only one of the dealer's cards. Each card is valued at its numerical identity and all face cards are counted as 10. The ace may be counted as 1 or 11. If a player "hits" and the total value of the cards exceeds 21, the player loses and the dealer takes the bet. This is referred to as a "bust." A player may receive as many cards as desired, and, once satisfied with the total, "stays." Players are not allowed to touch the cards or the bet, once play begins. To signal a hit, the player will generally be expected to brush his fingers on the table behind the cards or say, "Hit me." When the player wants no more cards, he waves his hand over the cards or says, "Stay." Each player, in turn, goes through the same decision process. The dealer plays last and is required to follow specific rules, regardless of the value of the players' hands. If the dealer's two-card value is less than 17, he or she must hit. If the total is 17 or over, the dealer must stay unless the 17 is made up of an ace and 6 (soft 17), which must be hit. Let's assume that the dealer has a 10 and an 8, for a total of 18. Everyone with 18 ties the dealer (a push), and no money is exchanged. Those with less than 18 lose the bet and those with over 18 win their bets. After the winners are paid, the players make their next bet. If the dealer's hand exceeds 21, all players that haven't busted win, regardless of the hand totals.

One of the options mentioned is "splitting." When a player receives two cards of the same value, he or she may treat each card as a separate hand. This is done by putting up another bet equal to the original bet and telling the dealer to split. The split bet is placed alongside the original bet. The dealer will physically move the cards so they are side by side and will follow the player's directions in regard to hitting and standing. The player receives cards on one card at a time until it is "good," or busts. The other split card is then played out as the first. When splitting, a player may take as many cards as desired except when splitting aces. Today's rules only allow the player to receive one card on each ace. If the first card received on a split is the same value as the split card, the cards may be split again. Aces, however, may only be split once. If the first card received on a split hand brings the total to 10 or 11 the player may "double-down."

The double-down is allowed if the value of any first two cards equals 10 or 11. To double, the player places an additional wager, up to the amount of the original bet, behind the original bet and tells the dealer to double. Note that it is not mandatory to match the original wager. It is, however, desirable to do so. The player receives only one card face up on a double-down bet.

Receipt of a 10-value card and an ace on the deal is referred to as a blackjack or natural. The player automatically beats the dealer unless the dealer also receives a blackjack. The player receives 3/2 on the bet for a blackjack. In other words, if a player bets $10 on the hand, he or she will receive $15 for the natural. The dealer receives no bonus for having a natural. Keep in mind that a blackjack is only paid 3/2 on the first two cards. Split hands and double-downs cannot become blackjacks.

Dealers seldom look at their hole (down) card in today's game until all players have completed play. At one time, it was a common practice for the dealer to peek when an ace or 10-value card was up. When the dealer had a natural it would be turned up immediately and the dealer would take all bets (except pushes). This practice was terminated because "experts" could gain information by the way the dealer looked at the hole card and by small bends put in the cards while looking under. When a 4 was the hole card, a second look was often required by the dealer to determine it wasn't an ace. There was a temptation by some dealers to look at the hole card when not required to do so. This raised the question of possible cheating. A natural by the dealer in today's game will usually not be known until all players have completed their turn. If the dealer has a blackjack, the players who doubled-down or split will only lose their original bets.

When the dealer's up card is an ace, the players will be asked if they want insurance. Taking insurance is betting that the dealer's hole card is a 10 or picture card, giving the dealer a natural. The cost of insurance is up to 1/2 of the original bet and returns 2/1 if the dealer has the natural. If the player's bet was $10, he or she could insure for up to $5 and receive back $10 if the dealer has the natural. The players then lose the initial bet due to the dealer's natural, unless he or she possessed one as well. When the dealer has the natural, the players who take insurance come out even. Those who decide not to take the insurance lose their bets. The players with a blackjack push on the hand and make 2/1 on the insurance bet. Taking insurance when one has a natural is a sure way of netting a profit. If the dealer does not have the 10 in the hole, all players lose the insurance bet and the dealer finishes play to determine the outcome of the original bets. In this case, some players will lose the insurance and the original bet!

It should be obvious that a player never wants to bust! The problem is, when a dealer has a 7 or higher showing, odds are the dealer has a "standing hand" and will not bust. When the dealer has a 7-through-ace up, all players should hit until they reach 17 or higher. When a dealer has a bust card up (2-6), the player should stay on 12 or more and make the dealer hit. Exceptions to this play strategy are found in the Winning Play Strategy chapter.

Many players haven't the foggiest idea of what they are doing. I have seen players stop on a total of 7. This is absolutely crazy! No card could possibly hurt the hand. Regardless of the dealer's up card, always hit, split, or double if the total is less than 12! There are many players who never take a hit if their total is 12 or more, regardless of the dealer's up card. This strategy may result in winning a few hands but is giving the casino a tremendous advantage overall. Some players will play exactly backward. These guys stay on 12-16 when the dealer has a standing card up and hit on 12-16 when the dealer has a stiff up. They seem to understand that there is something significant about 12-16 but are missing the big picture. As they say, a little bit of knowledge can be dangerous!

What confuses many novice players is that the ace may be counted as a 1 or 11. When the ace is counted as 11 we have what is called a "soft hand." A hand consisting of ace/6 can be counted as a 7, or a soft 17. When the ace must be counted as 1, in order to avoid exceeding 21, it is part of a "hard hand." A hand consisting of ace/6/6 is a hard 13.

The player who always bets the same amount, never splits or doubles, will almost certainly go home broke. The casino will normally win more hands than the player. This is guaranteed by the fact that the dealer is always last to play. When the players bust, the dealer takes the money regardless of what eventually happens to the dealer's hand. Busting should not be avoided by never taking hits on "stiff hands" (12-16). Such strategy gives the house an even larger advantage. To beat the casino at blackjack, one must win more money on fewer hands. This is accomplished through a progression betting scheme, and by taking advantage of all double-down and split situations. Knowing when to hit and stand is not enough. In the chapters to follow I will discuss, in detail, the best play strategy, betting progressions and money management to enable you to beat the casino.

Be prepared to run into all types of people at a blackjack table. About half of them will claim to be "experts," the other half will gladly admit that they know nothing about the game. I get the biggest kick from watching the constant mood swings that transpire as the luck turns. I have seen plump jolly men turn into raving lunatics as the cards began to fall the wrong way. You will most certainly run into the character who wants to tell everyone what to do. I wonder why these guys' chips are always going down if they know so much!

The card counter can usually be found sitting in one of the corner seats. The preferred domain will be the last seat to the dealer's right, which is often referred to as "the anchor" or "third base." From there, the counter gets a better view of all the cards and makes the last play before the dealer. This enables the counter to see more cards before his or her play. At times you will probably notice one or two spectators gazing over your shoulder. These are often counters, casing the shoe for the right time to enter the game.

Remember, you are at the table to have a good time. There is nothing wrong with taking advantage of the free drinks and casual conversation. Just don't have such a good time that you make mistakes in your play or betting. If you order drinks it is customary to tip the waitress; she will gladly accept chips. As you win, try and be a good sport about it. Your playing partners don't really care to hear what an expert you are. Try your best to refrain from telling others how to play. This is quite often a hard thing to avoid, particularly when people are staying on 12 against a dealer's 10.

Tipping the dealer is allowed. If the dealer gives you a great run or good shoe, think about giving an appropriate tip. The dealer will be just as happy if you make an extra wager on the hand for him or her. Do not blame a run of bad luck on the dealer. They have nothing to gain by taking your money. It is just the current luck of the cards. I get tired of listening to people giving the dealer a hard time. If you're unlucky at a table, move to another. Dealers do get lucky and often get on "hot streaks."

There will be times when the players preceding you will hit when they shouldn't and take the cards that would have helped you. Keep your cool. Others have as much right to play as you do, no matter how bad their play may be. You will really have to take it in stride when the dealer has a 5 card up and the anchor man hits a 14, takes the dealer's bust card, causing you to lose. Don't feel obligated to inform the anchor man of his blunder—someone will beat you to it! You will tend to always remember these situations. Keep in mind, just as many player mistakes work to your advantage.

If amateur play upsets you, the percentage of beginners at the table can be reduced by going to a table with a higher minimum required bet. Of course, your financial situation must be able to support the move. If you encounter a dealer who is unfriendly, or just a plain jerk, move to another table. It is not worth the aggravation. After all, you are there to enjoy yourself as well as make money.

2

A Winning Play Strategy

It takes four elements to win at blackjack. They are:

1. Proper play based on mathematical probabilities.
2. Proper betting with a progression system.
3. Proper money management.
4. Luck!

A good blackjack player requires discipline and knowledge of the first three elements. He or she does not have to rely as heavily on luck, as does the average player, to beat the dealer. In many ways good players make their own luck through proper play and progressive bets. To the onlookers, the good player appears to be lucky, but in actuality, is only playing the percentages.

The most widely accepted play strategies are based on the original computer calculations done by Julian Braun of IBM. Every teacher of blackjack strategy varies slightly from his findings. Some strategies are bolder and more aggressive then Mr. Braun's; others are more conservative. The strategy that I recommend is based on a cumulation of computer studies, numerous blackjack books and personal experience at the tables.

Obtaining a higher total without exceeding 21, or forcing the dealer to bust, is the goal of proper play. Having knowledge of only one dealer's card requires that actions taken be based on mathematical probability. By adhering to "winning strategy," discounting "hunches" and "feelings," the player gains a slight mathematical advantage over the dealer. While the dealer must obey strict hitting and standing rules, the player does not. Play strategy is a self-imposed set of player rules.

Hard Hitting and Standing

To hit or stand is a fundamental decision. This decision is made more often than any other. Luckily, this is the easiest strategy to learn. If the dealer's up card is a "standing card" (7-A), hit until your total is 17 or greater. When the dealer's up card is a "stiff" (2-6), do not hit if your total is 13 or more. If your total is 12, hit when the dealer's up card is a 2 or 3. This may seem risky, but, believe me, the odds are in your favor to hit the 12 against a 2 or 3! In a deck of 52 cards only 16 10-value cards are available to cause you to bust, 20 cards help (5, 6, 7, 8, 9), and 16 cards that can't hurt (A, 2, 3, 4). In other words, the odds are approximately 70 percent that the "hit" will help, or at least, not hurt. On the other hand, with a 2 or 3 up, the dealer has a good hand to hit to, regardless of the hole card. Once your total is 13 or more, stay!

Most blackjack players always stay on 12 when the dealer has a stiff card up. As I have explained, that strategy is contrary to mathematical probability, and is not proper play. Expect the table "experts" to criticize your play as you hit to 12 against the dealer's 2 or 3. Let them rave on about how lucky you were to have received a 9 for 21 instead of busting. You will never be able to convince the know-it-alls that your play was correct. Don't waste your time by trying. Be content in the knowledge that you and the dealer understand percentages! Please, when you *do* bust (which will happen), don't start to doubt the proper play.

The hard hitting and standing strategy is quite simple to remember. By assuming that the dealer has a 10-value card in the hole (though the odds are against it!), with a standing card up (7-A), figure the dealer for a standing hand and hit until you have a hard 17 or greater. Do not risk exceeding 21 when the dealer has the potential to bust, unless your total is 12, and the dealer has a 2 or 3 up.

Keep in mind, all house rules require the dealer hit to 17 or more.

The casinos would not require this unless it was to their advantage. In all cases, when the dealer has a standing card showing, follow the same rules as the casino. When the dealer has a bust card up, take advantage, and give the dealer the chance to bust. The percentages are in your favor. Make sure that you always hit, split or double-down on hands that are 11 or less.

I know of players willing to stay on a total of 9 if the dealer has a stiff up. Their thinking is, the dealer will bust; why hit?

This kind of thinking has put millions of dollars in the casino's coffers. Always hit hands that are less than 12, regardless of the dealer's up card! It is impossible to bust these hands and can only help.

Hit those 15's and 16's against dealer's standing cards. You will most likely bust, but may get lucky and receive a good hit. If you decide not to hit, expect to lose more hands overall. Let's face it, a stiff against a dealer's standing card is a losing proposition. Proper play will help to minimize the number of losses in this situation.

Soft Hitting and Standing

Soft hands often confuse the average player. I have actually observed players staying on soft 15's and 16's! These players might just as well give their money to the casino's cashier and leave. As a whole, the soft hands are misplayed more than any other hand in the game of blackjack.

House rules almost always require that the dealer hit a soft 17 and stay on hard 17 or above. Once again, the advantage is to follow the house.

Always hit a soft 17, regardless of the dealer's up card! If you receive a 10-value card, the hand becomes a hard standing 17. The 2, 3, or 4 significantly improves the hand. An ace makes the hand a standing 18, unless the dealer's up card is a 9 or 10, which requires another hit. If the hit hurts (5, 6, 7, 8, 9), the hand may still be improved by taking another card. With a 62 percent chance of hitting to a hard 17 or improving the hand, a player is crazy not to hit the soft 17's. Particularly when the player has a second chance to improve the hand if the hit card hurts. There are times that this strategy will turn what would have been a push with the dealer into a player bust. The overall gains will far override the losses.

As mentioned in the preceding paragraph, hit a soft 18 against a dealer's up card of 9 or 10. The average dealer standing hand is over 18. A soft 17 is not a good hand and a soft 18 does not fare well against a dealer's up card of 9 or 10. Through my research, which included thousands of hands dealt, hitting a soft 18 against a 9 or 10 was beneficial 62 percent of the time. Always stand with a soft 19 or 20!

Hard Double-Down

Taking advantage of double-down opportunities is an absolute necessity! The player who is afraid to double-down is throwing away a tremendous player advantage. Years ago, all casinos allowed players to double-down on any two cards. This practice was terminated when the casinos got wise to the degree in which the players gained an advantage. In today's game, players are usually only allowed to double-down on 10 or 11. Casinos would do away with the double-down option entirely but fear the decrease in business this would cause.

It is still possible to find a casino that allows players to double-down on any two cards. For this reason, I will discuss other double-down options later in the chapter. Many authors tend to give the impression that most casinos offer double-down on any two cards, which is not the case. Only in Nevada will you find such casinos.

The winning play strategy for double-downs is quite simple. Always double-down on 11. Double-down on 10 against all dealer up cards except a 10-value card. The double-down gives the player two chances to beat the dealer. The odds are good of receiving a high-value card and beating the dealer's standing hand. On the other hand, when the player receives a low-value card, he or she can still win if the dealer busts.

Most players never double-down against a dealer's ace. This strategy is not smart. If the dealer has a natural, the player only loses the original bet and receives back the double-down bet. I like to double against the ace because I know for sure that I will not be competing with a 10-value card in the hole. I believe the main reason people do not double against the ace is because they don't understand the rules.

You should not double a 10 against a dealer's 10-value card up. The odds are just not in your favor. Hit the 10, as per the hard hitting strategy. Some experts disagree with doubling 11 against the dealer's 10-value card. They are wrong! The odds favor doubling on the 11 against any card the dealer may have up.

A player must be prepared to lose double-down hands. I guarantee that if you follow my strategy you will win more hands than you lose. Always wager the maximum allowed on the double, which is the value of the original bet. Never be afraid to double, regardless of the bet size. If your bet is $500, go for it! Again I stress, don't let intuition or feelings get in the way of the correct play (unless you're a psychic!).

In many ways, I prefer to double on 10 as opposed to 11. I hate it when the ace is dropped on the 11 giving me a 12! On the other hand, the ace on my 10 is a pretty sight. Don't get upset when you receive a poor hit. Maintain a positive attitude and watch the dealer bust. Ideally, the double situations occur when the dealer's up card is a stiff. If given the opportunity, I would bet the table limit on all doubles against a stiff. Receiving a high-value card on a double, against a stiff, is icing on the cake.

Soft Double-Down

As stated earlier, casinos that allow players to double-down on any two cards are available. These casinos should be sought out and taken advantage of. The option of doubling down on any two cards is to the player's advantage. In Chapter 1, I mentioned that there were casinos with more liberal rules in favor of the player; this is what I was referring to.

You will notice that I only recommend doubling down on soft hands, when the dealer's up card is a stiff (2-6). This strategy relies as heavily on the dealer busting as it does on the player's hand being improved. When double-down is not recommended, play the hand as described under "soft hitting and standing."

Soft 13 (A-2)

Double-down on soft 13 against a dealer's up card of 4, 5 or 6. With 49 unseen cards left in a deck of 52 (the A-2 and 4, 5 or 6 are in play), the chance of improving the soft 13 with a 4, 5, 6, 7 or 8 is 19/49; approximately 39 percent. Any other card received results in a total of less than 17. To your advantage, the odds are good that the dealer will bust. In other words, you may receive a good standing hand, but are primarily betting that the dealer is going to bust! It is important to only double against the 4, 5, or 6, to ensure the dealer has a better-than-average chance of busting.

I used the example of one deck of cards for simplicity's sake. Regardless of the number of decks used, the odds are about the same. Obviously, the ratios change as cards are removed from the shoe. The 39% cited is based on random distribution and provides only a feel for the percentage of times you should expect your hand to improve.

Soft 14, 15, 16 (A-3, 4, 5)

As with the soft 13, double-down against the dealer's up card of 4, 5 or 6. Once again, only double against the dealer's three worst possible up cards. The strategy is the same as for the soft 13. You can easily determine the cards which will help, and the odds of such a hit.

Soft 17, 18 (A-6, 7)

Double-down on a soft 17 or 18 against a dealer's up card of 3, 4, 5 or 6. The strategy is similar to the previous soft double situations. Receiving a 10-value card on the soft 17 and 18 results in hard hands of 17 and 18, respectively. This added advantage accounts for expanding the dealer's required up card to include the 3. Some strategies allow players to double against a 2. I have hound the 2 to be a dangerous card to hit against. With a 2 up, the dealer has an above-average chance of hitting to a standing hand.

Soft 19, 20 (A-8,9)

Never double-down on soft 19 or 20! These are strong hands and are too difficult to improve. Be happy with winning the bet and don't get greedy. As I have previously mentioned, the dealer's average standing hand is slightly over 18. You have that beat!

Other Double-Down Situations

9

Double-down on a two-card total of 9 against all stiffs (2-6). The chance of hitting to a standing hand of 17 through 20 is approximately 56%. This in itself puts the odds in your favor. For added insurance, the requirement that the dealer's up card be a stiff makes this an excellent bet.

8

Double-down on an 8 against a dealer's up card of 5 or 6 only. This is a borderline double-down, but the odds are in the player's favor. With fewer "helping" cards available, only double against one of the two worst possible dealer up cards.

The last time my wife, Robin, and I were in Vegas we found a casino downtown (off the Strip) which offered double-down on any two cards. We took advantage of the liberal rules and made a hefty profit at the tables. Every chance we had, we doubled. The percentages went our way and we won the majority of the doubles.

I was surprised that the casino was not crowded. In fact, there was hardly anyone at the tables. The majority of the players were in the larger, better known casinos. I am perfectly willing to sacrifice the glitz for the gold! Obviously, John Q. Public is unaware of the advantage double-downs offer. I would hope, after reading this book, that you will seek out and play at such casinos.

When I travel to Reno or Las Vegas on a casino "package deal" I make sure that I spend the required time at the "host" casino's tables to qualify for all benefits and thus ensure that I am invited back. These benefits are often as much as $200 in cash and "play" coupons. I subsequently find the casino in town with the most liberal blackjack rules. I highly recommend this procedure for anyone who plays blackjack to win!

Splitting Pairs

Another key factor in the quest to beat blackjack is the proper splitting of pairs. Very few experts agree on what pairs to split, and when. Some players always split pairs; this strategy is a sure road to disaster.

In some cases, pairs are split with the intent of winning both hands. Some pairs are split to avoid a bust, with the possibility of winning both hands, but a more realistic expectation of breaking even (win one, lose the other). Never should a pair be split if likely to lose both hands. Nor should a pair be split if it requires breaking up a winning hand. This criteria is the basis behind the winning strategy of splitting pairs.

Aces

Always split aces! The chances of winning both hands are excellent, regardless of the dealer's up card. An 11 is a much better total to hit to than a 2. The only drawback is that you only receive one card on a split ace. With only one hit the odds are approximately 64 percent that each ace will reach a total of 17 or more.

Splitting aces is similar to doubling down, since each only receives one card. Most of the time you can expect to win both hands, some of the time you will only win one hand and break even on the bet. A very small percentage of the time should you expect to lose both hands. Splitting aces is a very good bet. All knowledgeable players advocate splitting aces.

10

Never split 10's! 20 is a winning hand and should never be split up. Why take a winner and risk turning it into a loser? Some casinos allow players to split picture cards even if they don't match—isn't that nice of them! The splitting of 10's is idiotic!

As you may have guessed, I get emotional about splitting 10's. Of all bonehead plays, this takes the cake. I have yet to go on a gambling trip and not see players splitting 10's. Their logic must be that both 10's will become 20. Wrong! Only 16 of every 52 cards is a 10 value card (31 percent). I keep it to myself but get very upset when I see a player split 10's and end up with a 17 and a bust hand against a dealer's 18. Some dealers are nice enough to inform such players of the error in their ways. The players don't listen and try again!.

Years ago there was a time and place for splitting 10's ("end play" discussed in Systems chapter). In today's game a player never encounters a situation that benefits by splitting 10's. Be happy to win the hand with the 20 and move on to the next hand.

9

Split 9,s against 2 through 9. Do not split against 10 or ace. This split is made with the expectation of winning both hands against a dealer's 2-8 and to win or break even against the 9. As stated earlier, the average dealer standing hand is slightly over 18. The pair of 9's is therefore not a strong hand.

Splitting against the 10 or ace is not wise. This would most likely result in losing two hands. Stand, and hope the dealer loses the hand but don't risk doubling your losses. The dealer will most likely win the hand with your 18 up against their 10 or ace.

Some experts recommend not splitting the 9 against 7. The argument is that the dealer has a 17 and the split will be breaking up a winning hand. I don't buy this. There is only about a 30 percent chance of a 10 or face card in the hold. Though we always assume a 10-value card in the hole for hitting purposes, let's not get carried away. Split that 9 and win both hands!

8's

Split 8's against 2 through 8. Most strategies disagree and preach always splitting 8's. The generally accepted belief is that 16 is a terrible hand that must be split to avoid a bust. My argument is, why lose double? Take the hit against dealer's 9-A, and hope for the best. Hitting an 8 against a dealer's 9, 10 or ace is a losing proposition.

I am fighting the computers on this one, but have years of experience to back my argument. I have yet to see the computer lose money on a bet. For years I always split 8's, and for years I lost my shirt when up against the dealer's 9, 10 or ace.

Splitting 8's against 2-8 is obviously a smart play. The intent is to take a terrible hand and turn it into two winners. It works!

7's

Split 7's against 2 through 7. Against the 2-6 I expect to win both hands. Against the 7 I hope to at least come out even. 14 is not a good hand to hit. Grit your teeth and hit against dealer's 8-A, don't split and turn the hand into two losers!

6's

Split 6's against 2 through 6. The odds are better to split the 6's against a 2 or 3 than to hit and risk a bust, as per the hard hitting and standing strategy. Against the 4, 5 and 6 there is an excellent chance that the dealer will bust, resulting in two winning hands. Hit against standing cards but never split against them. The 6 is a miserable card to hit.

5's

Never split 5's. With a total of 10, double-down is warranted. 10 is a great hand to hit. Don't screw it up and split, regardless of the dealer's up card.

4's

Split 4's against dealer's up card of 5 or 6. In this case there is a very good chance of the dealer busting. Most authors recommend doubling down against the 5 or 6, which is not allowed in many casinos throughout the world. Hit to the 8 against all other cards. Some experts argue that 4's should never be split. Come on, 8 is not a strong card to hit to and a 5 and 6 are the worst possible dealer up cards.

2's and 3's

Split 2's and 3's against 2 through 7. These are good splits to hit to. Don't let the dealer's 7 up card scare you. The percentages are on your side.

Stay alert at all times. Remember that if the first card on a split gives a total that qualifies for a double-down, take advantage if allowed. If you receive a like card on a split, split again.

Recently at the tables, while betting $50, I split a pair of 3's against a dealer's 6. The first card received was another 3 which I again split. Without going into all of the detail, I continued to receive more 3's and ended up with 5 hands in play. Two of the hands were a 10 and 11 which I doubled down on. With $350 now in play, I felt as though I had hit a grand slam, as the dealer busted!

Insurance

We are taught from day one that insurance is one of life's necessities. You would not dare (I hope) drive your car without it. Most of us carry life insurance and all of us have home or rental insurance. We pay all of our lives and hope we never collect. What a losing proposition that is!

By offering insurance, the casino's knew they would have takers. After all, insurance is necessary. The use of the word "insurance" was marketing genius. I see players knocking over their chips in a panic to get their insurance money on the table.

The insurance bet can only be made when the dealer's up card is an ace. The player may bet up to half of the original bet and wagers that the dealer has a 10 or picture card in the hole. The idea is to insure your hand in case the dealer has a natural. The player breaks even by winning the insurance bet and losing the original bet (unless the player also has a natural) on the dealer's blackjack.

Do you really believe that insurance is an advantage for the player? I hate to be the one to spill the beans, but insurance is a casino moneymaker! It sounds great. The player gets 2/1 on the bet and doesn't lose a penny on the hand when the dealer has the blackjack. After all, we are taught to assume that the dealer has a 10 in the hole. What you're not told is that the chance of a 10-value card in the hole is actually about 1/2.5.

The casino is willing to give us 2/1 on a 2.5/1 bet. Isn't that nice of them! It becomes even more interesting when you realize that the casino never has to put up a penny of its own money on this bet! The player already has money on the table. If the natural occurs, the dealer pays with the player's own money. If the 10 is *not* in the hole, the dealer takes the insurance bet and play continues.

In the long run, taking insurance is throwing money away. Most of the time you will lose the insurance bet. Assume you bet $10 on the hand. After insuring for $5, and losing, the most you can make is $5 if your hand beats the dealer's. In other words, you have given half of your winnings away. If the hand is lost, you lose more than was originally bet. Some players always take insurance; they need someone to straighten them out. Against a dealer's ace up is not the time to risk more money on your hand.

I must admit that I advocate taking insurance when the player has a blackjack. Though it goes against the odds, it is a *guaranteed* profit, and I'm not one to throw a sure thing away. Assuming $50 is bet, insurance will cost $25. If the dealer has the natural, I collect $50 on the insurance and push on the hand, the net profit being $50, the original bet. If the dealer does not have the natural, I lose the insurance but collect $75 for the blackjack. Again, a net profit of $50.

My insurance strategy is to ignore it unless I have a blackjack. Taking insurance on the natural is the only time I go against the odds. Can you blame me?

Summary

Playing the odds is the best "long run" strategy. I have never met a winning player who ignores proper play strategy. Minor deviations from accepted strategies will not significantly hurt one's chances of success. Be consistent in the play, however. If you choose to split 8's against the dealer's 9 (against my recommendation), do it every time. Once you begin to vary the play from one moment to another you are no longer playing the odds. In fact, you will be guessing/playing on intuition, which does not work.

For your convenience, my Winning Play Strategy is summarized in tables 2.1-2.4. You should learn this strategy through practice as I describe in the Home Improvement chapter. As I previously mentioned, I have at times detoured from the majority of the experts' beliefs (i.e., I do not recommend always splitting 8's).

To play winning blackjack, never deviate from the following basic strategies:

1. Never split 5's, 10's or face cards!
2. Always split aces!
3. Always hit to a hard 17, or greater, against the dealer's standing card!
4. Always hit, split, or double-down on hands totaling less than 12!
5. Always hit a soft 17!
6. Never hit a 13-16 against a dealer's stiff!

In addition to the preceding strategy, you must also take advantage of all split and double-down situations. Failure to capitalize on these opportunities will make the difference between winning and losing!

HARD HAND PLAY STRATEGY

DEALER'S UP CARD

	2	3	4	5	6	7	8	9	10	A
17-20	S	S	S	S	S	S	S	S	S	S
13-16	S	S	S	S	S	H	H	H	H	H
12	H	H	S	S	S	H	H	H	H	H
11	D	D	D	D	D	D	D	D	D	D
10	D	D	D	D	D	D	D	D	H	D
9	*	*	*	*	*	H	H	H	H	H
8	H	H	H	*	*	H	H	H	H	H
5-7	H	H	H	H	H	H	H	H	H	H

S = STAND   H = HIT   D = DOUBLE
* = DOUBLE IF PERMITTED/OTHERWISE HIT

PLAYER'S HAND

SOFT HAND PLAY STRATEGY

DEALER'S UP CARD

	2	3	4	5	6	7	8	9	10	A
A9	S	S	S	S	S	S	S	S	S	S
A8	S	S	S	S	S	S	S	S	S	S
A7	S	+	+	+	+	S	S	H	H	S
A6	H	*	*	*	*	H	H	H	H	H
A5	H	H	*	*	*	H	H	H	H	H
A4	H	H	*	*	*	H	H	H	H	H
A3	H	H	*	*	*	H	H	H	H	H
A2	H	H	*	*	*	H	H	H	H	H

S=STAND   H=HIT
+=DOUBLE IF PERMITTED/OTHERWISE STAY
*=DOUBLE IF PERMITTED/OTHERWISE HIT

PLAYER'S HAND

DOUBLE-DOWN PLAY STRATEGY

DEALER'S UP CARD

	2	3	4	5	6	7	8	9	10	A
11	D	D	D	D	D	D	D	D	D	D
10	D	D	D	D	D	D	D	D		D
9	D	D	D	D	D					
8				D	D					
A2			D	D	D					
A3			D	D	D					
A4			D	D	D					
A5			D	D	D					
A6		D	D	D	D					
A7		D	D	D	D					

PLAYER'S HAND

SPLITTING PAIRS PLAY STRATEGY

DEALER'S UP CARD

	2	3	4	5	6	7	8	9	10	A
AA	S	S	S	S	S	S	S	S	S	S
1010	F	O	R	G	E	T		I	T	!
99	S	S	S	S	S	S	S	S		
88	S	S	S	S	S	S	S			
77	S	S	S	S	S	S				
66	S	S	S	S	S					
55	F	O	R	G	E	T		I	T	!
44				S	S					
33	S	S	S	S	S	S				
22	S	S	S	S	S	S				

PLAYER'S HAND

3

Systems

As a serious blackjack player, I have studied and tested numerous "systems" and strategies over the past twenty years. I have spent hundreds of hours developing card counting skills, through practice and under actual battle conditions in the casinos. I have tested these systems in Reno, Las Vegas, Atlantic City, the Bahamas and aboard cruise ships. In addition, hundreds of hours have been spent testing on computers and against my wife, as dealer, at home.

With very few exceptions, systems today are a photocopy of Dr. Edward Thorp's point count system, with minor adjustments to allegedly compensate for today's rules and multiple-deck use. The strategies, betting recommendations and money management techniques are all very similar from one book/video to another. Each "expert" throws in some minor but insignificant modification to make his system "unique."

After careful study and years of testing, I have concluded that the experts must profit from their teachings because there is not much chance of making money from their systems. There are no miracle systems that give the player a significant advantage over the house. Most systems fail to ensure that larger bets are made while on a winning streak, which is the key to making a profit. The card counting systems only tell the player to bet more when the "chance" of winning a particular hand is to his advantage. With multiple decks and quick shuffles, however, the instances when a player has a significant advantage are scarce.

The Martingale System

The Martingale system, also known as the negative progression or double-up system, is based on the theory that if one is allowed to double-up after each losing hand, he or she should never lose! After all, a player must eventually win a hand. This, my friend, is the reason there are wagering limits on all the gaming tables.

A small percentage of players still believe in the double-up system despite the table limits. They gamble on winning a hand before the limit is reached. Let's assume the table limit is $200 and the player's bet is $10. The negative progression bettor will bet and win $10, until a loss. At such time, $20 would be bet. If the bet is won, the next bet reverts back to $10. If lost, it goes to $40. At first appearance the system looks great! Gaining ten bucks every few minutes is nothing to sneeze at. But what happens if the dealer wins several in a row? The betting sequence would be: $10-$20-$40-$80-$160. After losing only five hands in a row, the player's next bet would have to be $320, which exceeds the table limit. The player cannot possibly recoup the losses in this run of bad luck because of the limit! The example does not even take into account that the player may have lost a split or double-down situation during the losing streak, to compound the loss. The Martingale system is for suckers! Dealers always manage to have streaks that are devastating to this betting system.

At a table in Atlantic City I observed a high roller using this system. He was extremely lucky and was ahead thousands. of dollars. The table limit was $500 and his minimum bet was $25. I was barely holding my own using a point count system at the time. I had read somewhere that the double-up system was suicidal, so I was amazed to see it work so well. To be honest, I was somewhat envious of all the money he was making. I was almost starting to believe that his system could actually work for me. After all, he didn't have to count cards to determine his bet. He was having a great time, making money and drinking free booze. I was having to work hard at concentrating on the cards and could not drink for fear of losing the required sharpness. The table in front of him was stacked with $25 and $100 chips. I couldn't believe his good fortune. He would lose a few hands in a row, double-up each time, and ultimately win. He would often have to make a $200 bet, be dealt a double-down situation, and win $400. I couldn't stand it any longer and asked him what would happen if he lost several in a row. He made it very clear to me that the odds of losing more than five in a row were slim to none. As they say, "All good things must come to an end"; his luck changed. The dealer had a run of unbeatable luck. The player rapidly reached the table limit and proceeded to lose all of his winnings. I saw the panic in his eyes as he lost $1,000 while splitting aces. According to the "count," we should have been doing well. The dealer kept getting the good hits, 20 hands, and blackjacks. Mr. Double-Up didn't know what to do. He would bet the maximum in an effort to recoup his losses, continue to lose and ultimately drop back to his minimum bet of $25. He would win an occasional bet but eventually reach the table limit. I should have quit playing at that table because the dealer was "hot." I had to stick around to see if the double-up system could survive. I felt guilty for mentioning the possibility of such a dealer streak, as I watched the stacks of chips disappear. Ultimately, Mr. Double-Up lost all of his winnings and kicked in about $800 of his own money. I had witnessed one of the most dramatic turnabouts that I have ever seen. There was no longer any doubt in my mind: the negative progression has moments of success but will always get you in the end!

Counting Fives

One of the very first systems touting a mathematical advantage over the casino was based on counting fives. Statistically, if a deck is short of 5's, the advantage goes to the player. In a single-deck game the advantage was calculated to be as high as 3.6 percent. This is not a significant advantage and would not tempt me to throw a massive bet onto the table!

To take maximum advantage of this system, players were encouraged to bet "high" when all 5's were removed from the deck. The advantage of 5's being removed has to do with increasing the chances of the dealer busting. The player only had to monitor 5's and base his bets and hard hitting numbers on the ratio of unseen cards over unseen 5's (unseen cards/unseen 5's). This required the player to track 5's, count cards and divide continuously. The calculated ratio determined the bet to be made and sometimes required deviation from standard play strategy.

I know of no one who uses this system today. I find it very hard to believe that it could have ever been successful. With multiple-deck games the chances of ever having an advantage is slim to none. I have never considered using this system and only include it in this chapter because it was used by the "experts" before the more powerful counting systems were developed.

Counting Tens

The first truly effective system developed was based on counting tens. In fact, all current systems revolve around the theory that the richer a deck is in high-value cards, the larger the player advantage. When a dealer has a stiff card up (2-6) the chances of an actual bust are greatly increased if there is a high percentage of 10-value cards in the deck. When the deck is "rich" in tens and aces, the number of naturals a player can receive increases. The dealer may also receive more blackjacks, but is not paid 3/2, as is the player. Successful double-downs and splits are more likely when the deck is rich in 10's and picture cards.

The basic ten-count system requires the player to track the ratio of total cards left in the deck to the number of unseen 10-value cards (cards left/10's left). The player starts with 36/16 and simply counts down as cards are seen. As the deck becomes 10-rich, the ratio decreases from 2.25 (36/16) toward the ideal ratio of 1. As the ratio decreases, the player's bet increases.

In the early 1960s the "experts" would not hesitate to bet the table limit when the ratio reached certain values and modified basic play strategy based on that ratio. Jumping from a $10 base bet to a $500 bet was common. As the casinos became aware of these "counters," the dealers were instructed to shuffle when such a jump bet was made. To prevent recognition as a counter, players were taught not to increase their bets more than 3- to 5-fold. A $10 bettor would raise the bet to $50, at most, if the count warranted.

The "counters" made huge profits before the casinos countered with multiple decks and quick shuffles. "Old-timers" often tell stories of how they murdered the casinos. Most of the large sums won were the result of "end play." When all but a few cards were dealt from a deck the counters knew exactly what cards were left, giving them an unbeatable advantage. This was referred to as end play. One author described how he had received a blackjack and doubled down on it! The dealer had a 10-value card up, there were only a few cards left in the deck, and all were 10's and face cards. The author doubled on the natural, knowing that his total would be 21 and that the dealer had a 20. Thus, the author made 2/1 on his bet versus the 3/2 offered for a natural. Time after time similar situations arose. Before the rule changes came about, a player could double on any two cards (some casinos in Nevada still allow it today). A counter would not hesitate to double on a 6 count if the dealer had a stiff up with only 10-value cards left in the deck. Players would often split 10's and picture cards against the dealer's 9, or less, under the same conditions.

It is obvious that the card counter had a tremendous advantage. Once the cat was let out of the bag (*Beat the Dealer* by Dr. Edward O. Thorp), casino blackjack was changed forever. Today's experts still cling to counting systems as though they are as powerful as they once were. In an eight-deck game the count starts at 416/128 (still 2.25), but rarely decreases appreciably. There is no such thing as end play, which was the counter's greatest weapon. Today's players rarely see more than 2/3 of the total cards. If a single- or double-deck game is found, the players will get a shuffle anytime the odds are in their favor (the dealers know how to count too!), or anytime their bets reflect a significant advantage.

For years I believed in the counting systems and spent hundreds of hours practicing and playing. In the multiple-deck games the advantageous situations were few and far between. When I did raise my bet I would often have to hit to a stiff and bust. The dealer was just as likely to get the 10-value cards as I was. I memorized the numerous basic strategy charts and made play adjustments accordingly. The memorization was a waste of time since it was rare when the count required me to vary from basic play strategy. I kept telling myself that I would beat the casino. I was taught that a good count required a higher bet, thus more money for my blackjacks. Ironically, with multiple-deck games, the vast majority of naturals occur while at the minimum bet. This is because most of the bets based on the count are minimum! I did hone my skills at division, memorization and concentration, but I did not make much money! It's really kind of funny; if we worked as hard at our jobs as we have to work using a count system, we would all be the best in our fields. Never have I had to work so hard to make so little. Don't get me wrong, I did fairly well when the cards went my way (which had little to do with the count!).

The Point Count

The point-count system is merely a refinement of the 10-count system. In this system the player keeps track of all cards seen by assigning them a value. Aces, 10's, and face cards are worth -1, 2-6 are assigned +1, and 7-9 are worth 0. A complete deck/shoe has a total of 0. If the count were +9, the deck/shoe would contain 9 more high-value cards than low-value cards. The higher the + count, the richer the remaining deck(s) is/are in high cards. The significance of the plus or minus value varies with the number of remaining cards. An almost full shoe with a +9 is not as high-card rich as a near-empty shoe is with the same count. For this reason, to determine the actual worth of the shoe, one must divide the count value by the number of remaining cards. This ratio is most often referred to as the "index number." Again, the player is required to concentrate, memorize and divide. As with the 10-count, the favorable situations are minimal and carry no guarantees.

Every blackjack author and his brother now teach some variation of the point count. Many include computer studies with values given for the percentage advantage of various index values. I have yet to read a book or see a video where the expert explains that a high percentage advantage is quite rare. These authors must also believe that the majority of us are whizzes at division and can divide 12 by 375 and come up with the correct index. The authors who admit that most games are now multiple-deck do offer the player a system that requires dividing the count by the number of remaining decks. This gives a rougher index, but it sure cuts down on the math! Of course, we must now learn their bet-versus-index chart and deviation-from-basic-strategy charts. They even teach us how to estimate the number of remaining decks and sometimes offer training drills! If it seems that I'm sounding a bit sarcastic, maybe I am.

As with the 10-count systems, I became proficient with numerous variations of the point-count system. I even made up my own system and determined my own betting tables based on current index. To make a long story short, I had about the same results with the point count as I did with the 10-count. The problem with both systems is that they did not allow me to raise my bet during a hot streak. There were times when I won several hands in a row with terrible index values, and lost just as many hands in a row with great index values (and more money bet). The average player is usually willing to lose maybe $200 to $500 on a gambling trip. With this kind of bankroll, we are limited to bet the minimum of $5 when unfavorable and $10 when favorable. The only way the count systems will produce a substantial profit in the long run is to bet much higher under favorable conditions. That's not realistic with a limited bankroll. The gamblers who pioneered the count systems were able to make table-limit bets because they were backed by big money while testing their systems. I wish that today's authors would admit these facts and quit teaching systems to the average player with an average bankroll. These systems require large bets to benefit from them!

Shuffle and Shuffle Tracking

Now that the point system has been beaten to death by every blackjack player with a word processor, the "experts" and "professionals" are looking for new excuses to justify the inadequacies. You can now learn how the casinos teach dealers legal but questionable shuffling techniques to prevent players from winning. Then you can send in more money and take specific courses in evaluating shuffles and learning to cut to win.

The basic premise is that by grouping high cards together, the dealer reduces the player's percentage. By not allowing a random shuffle, the dealer defeats the point-count system (because it is based on a random shuffle). To counter this, the experts teach how to determine a poor shuffle, take maximum advantage of a good shuffle, and so on. I guess there would be no such thing as a triangle if it weren't for angles!

A book I studied recently made shuffle studies and tracking its major tool for beating today's game. The authors build their analysis around the premise that it takes up to 30 shuffles of a single deck to get a random shuffle. Ironically, my father sent me a recent newspaper article which details how two mathematicians have proven that a single deck of cards requires only 7 shuffles for total randomness. Now, how accurate can the book on shuffle-tracking be?

I believe there is some substance to the shuffle arguments, but not enough to be worth the effort. If you don't do well at a table, move. It's as simple as that!

Summary

If you want to spend many hours learning a point-count system, go for it! Do not expect to win a great deal of money and be prepared to work hard. Try and enjoy yourself at the tables, but don't forget the count. Ensure that your division and memorization is accurate, and shun the free booze. Make sure you camouflage your bets in a single- or double-deck game. Most of all, remember to have a good time!

Now, if you want a chance to make big bucks, never have to count, divide or memorize, and have a great time, learn my betting progressions in the next chapter!

4

A Winning Progression

Some years ago I read a gambling book titled *How to Win* by Mike Goodman, a professional gambler and casino executive. His approach to the game of blackjack was unique and controversial. He believed in winning money! He openly challenged any and all experts to back up their systems at his casino and offered them a chance to hold public debates. To the best of my knowledge, he had no takers.

Mr. Goodman opened my eyes to a completely new approach to the game of blackjack. Without specifically attacking the card counting systems, he made it clear that the key to profitable blackjack play was to never risk more than a minimal bet while losing, and to increase the bet while winning. This strategy, which seems too easy to believe, works! The card counting systems can then be discarded because they require that a player determine the bet based on a "count" or "index," with no relationship to winning or losing.

How to Win should be required reading for all potential gamblers. In addition to blackjack, Mr. Goodman covers poker, craps, horse racing, and roulette. His approach is simple and accurate, and he is chock-full of interesting stories and anecdotes. I have never met the man, nor am I in any way obligated to push his book. I am grateful to Mr. Goodman for putting me on the right

33

path toward the goal of beating the house. I do not agree with some aspects of his book, but credit him fully with debunking the card-counting systems. My play strategy is similar but deviates quite often at times. The betting progression that he advocates is significantly different from mine. I have had very good luck with his betting scheme, but feel I have developed a much more powerful system. The major advantage of my progression is smaller losses and greater profits in the "war zone," which I will discuss later.

The objective is to win money from the casino. The reason "systems" exist is to obtain this objective. Knowing the rules, when to hit, split, or double-down are only small parts of beating the casino. Most people use good strategy but still manage to lose. They make the same bet each and every time. The average Joe will take a couple of hundred dollars to the table and bet $5 or $10 on every hand. If this player has good luck, takes advantage of splits and double-downs, he or she may break even or leave the table a few dollars ahead. With a bankroll of a few hundred dollars the player will most likely go bust sooner or later. With a relatively small bank the card counters will have about the same results, despite the "advantage" assured them by the experts. To beat the house you must understand that the dealer will win the majority of the hands. Even the experts must admit that there is no way to avoid losing more hands than the dealer. The key is to make more money on the winning hands than is lost on the losing hands. This can only be assured by increasing the bet as you win.

I wish I had a dollar for every player who lost their total bankroll and could not understand why. Their luck was relatively good and they can remember hitting several blackjacks. In many cases they can boast of being ahead at one time. You can also bet that they had several good "shoes" and won several hands in a row. I have seen players betting $2 a hand win as many as ten hands in a row and walk away from the table broke.

There is nothing to lose and everything to gain by using a betting progression. I assure you that with my progression you will draw the attention of many a pit boss. But, unlike a counter, there is nothing the casino can do about it. The player who won ten hands in a row at $2 per hand made a profit of $18 to $38 (if all ten hands were doubled or split) after losing the eleventh hand. Using my progression, the minimum profit would be $36 with the potential profit of $262. The actual profit would be somewhere between these two figures. After studying the progression you will see where I get these numbers. The important point is that at no time do I risk losing more than my minimum bet, and as I raise the bet, I am playing on "house" money.

Upon studying Mr. Goodman's book, I was sure that blackjack could be beat. I practiced at home using his scheme and did fairly well. I found that "luck" runs in streaks. As long as I had an occasional run of winning hands, I turned a profit. I compared the betting scheme with the bets required by various counting systems and determined the progression to be superior. After being convinced that a betting scheme could work, I was off to Reno.

My very first experience with the progression was profitable! I had very little capital and stayed with the $2 tables. After an eight-hour session I had made a couple hundred dollars. At the time, I felt as though I had stumbled onto a "miracle" system. Over the years I have had streaks of hot and cold sessions. I began to lose enthusiasm for the system after a few losses. The problem is, Mr. Goodman's progression requires a player to win four hands in a row to see a profit on a given streak. It also results in a loss of money when every other hand is lost. The system racked up huge profits when several hands were won in a row. On occasions, when I had no long runs, my finances took a beating.

I was still convinced that the Goodman strategy was superior and taught his scheme to my friends. On one occasion, a few of us flew down to Freeport, in the Bahamas. A good friend of mine, named Dan, decided to try Mr. Goodman's advice at the craps table, while I made a beeline for the blackjack tables. The dealer was not letting me win more than four hands in a row. Today, I refer to the first four hands of a run as the "war zone." Needless to say, my bankroll was on the decline. In the Bahamas the minimum bet allowed is $5. A player cannot afford bad luck for very long. While I was locked in the heat of battle, I could hear the screams and cheers coming from the craps table area. After losing my established limit I wandered over to the craps table to check out the action. Dan *was* the action! He was not rolling the dice but he was making all the money. He had made some bold modifications to Mr. Goodman's system, started with a $5 bet and was up to $500. He had covered every number with $500 and had $500 in odds on the "line bet." I don't expect you to be familiar with the game of craps; I am just pointing out that Dan had over $3,000 riding on the table. Dan would only lose if a seven was rolled, which has a 6/36 chance. He was not the least bit worried about losing the money on the table. To reach the $500 bet he had made a great deal more than $3,000. He was extremely lucky, and the players kept avoiding the seven. Eventually a seven was rolled and all the money bet on the numbers went to the casino. I'm not sure exactly what Dan made on the "run," but he was able to buy a new car, with cash, a few weeks later. The sad part of this story is that the players who made all the "points" made very little money throughout the run. They bet $5 on each number and never raised their bets! Sound familiar?

I came to the conclusion that the ideal situation was to develop a betting progression that allows a player to make large sums of money during big runs and to minimize the losses in the "war zone." After five years of experimenting and testing I have done just that! My system has the player break even with the dealer during periods when the dealer and player alternate wins, and ensures a profit after winning two hands in a row. It also allows the player to jump to higher profits rapidly (using casino money) during hot streaks.

To beat the casino we must minimize our losses and maximize our winnings. The only sure way to do this is to raise the bet as we win. The player who lowers the bet as he or she wins is not playing with a full deck, if you know what I mean. The betting scheme works on all tables regardless of the minimum limit. The minimum bet must be made based on the amount of money you have to work with. Never take more money to the casinos than you are willing to lose, and always be prepared to lose. With an adequate bankroll to support your minimum bet, you will give the casino one hell of a fight. With proper play and a small amount of luck you should be able to take a piece of the casino home! For ease of discussion I will start with the $10 progression.

The $10 Progression

10-10-15-15-20-20-30-30-50-50-70-70-100-100

The first thing you should note is that the minimum bet is $10 and the maximum bet is $100. Bets are to be made in the order shown.

As soon as a bet is lost, revert back to the first bet of the sequence. The most you will ever lose is $10 at a time (unless you lose a split or double). On the other hand, you may be making as much as $200 on a split or double-down. After winning the first bet of $10, repeat it. This is to ensure that you lose no money if you were to lose every other hand. The third bet of $15 ensures a profit after winning two hands in a row ($20-$15 = $5). Assuming no splits or doubles, the profits after losing the indicated number hand are as follows:

2nd = even • 3rd = $5 • 4th = $20 • 5th = $30 • 6th = $50 • 7th = $60 • 8th = $90 • 9th = $100 • 10th = $150 11th = $180 • 12th = $250 • 13th = $290 • 14th = $390 • Add $100 for each additional hand.

The profits listed are the minimum based on no blackjacks, splits, or doubles. The fact is, your profits will be significantly greater because you will receive blackjacks, win doubles, and splits during the runs. The weakness with the progression, as listed, is that it is somewhat slow in reaching the large bets. To enable one to rapidly advance up the betting ladder the rules are as follows:

1. Upon receipt of 3/2 on a blackjack, skip one level of the progression. In other words, if you are betting your first $20 and receive $30, the next bet should be your first $30 bet in lieu of a second $20 bet. If 3/2 is received on a second $20 bet, the next bet would be your second $30, in lieu of the first $30. This may sound slightly confusing, but is important to follow. This "jump" enables the player to reach the larger bets as quickly as possible. It is very important to make as much money as you can during a streak.

2. Upon winning double on the bet, or more (possible if more than two cards are split), skip two levels unless the money you are risking is more than you just received. In that case, only skip one level. In other words, if you win double on your first $20, your next bet would be your second $30 (skipped second $20 and first $30). If you receive double on the second $30 bet, you would not skip to $70 because you would be risking more than you just made $60). Instead, jump one level and bet the second $50. Following this second rule will get you betting the big bucks in a hurry.

At first glance the betting progression looks slow and not very exciting. It is actually just the opposite. You will be surprised at how fast you will reach the $50 and $100 bets. On your way to these levels you will have accumulated significant profits. The pit boss will most likely be asking you to fill out little cards that request your name, profession, etc. You may be invited to a free dinner and possibly free accommodations. The casino will have a difficult time figuring out exactly what you are doing, particularly when you make the two level jumps. They may mistake you for a card counter. Who cares? All the pit boss knows for sure is that you are willing to make $100 bets, and double to $200, as the case may be.

What makes this system so exciting is being able to make $100 bets with no worry. After all, it's the casino's money you are risking! Another advantage to such a betting scheme is that you are definitely making the most of a favorable shoe. Regardless of the "count," you make money from a run. All the casino ever gets is your minimal bet, no matter how many hands you lose in a row. An excellent chance to make large profits and not have to count, divide, or memorize; sure sounds good to me.

In conjunction with the betting progression and skip-bet rules, a smart player must use proper play strategy and take advantage of all double/split situations. Do not be afraid to split/double on a $70 or $100 bet! Look at it as frosting on the cake. Remember that the splits and doubles are to your advantage and must be cashed in on. Sure, you will lose some of these bets; thats why they call it gambling! Follow the system and be sure to drop back to the minimum bet after a loss. Do not get carried away with the winnings and decide to bet the same bet again after a loss. If you make a good deal of money and you want to increase profits, go to a higher betting progression; but don't vary from the scheme!

A few years ago, I was playing a similar betting progression in Las Vegas. I was doing quite well, even though the system was weaker in the "war zone." Apparently the count was very good, mostly low cards had been played. I noticed a young man about 25 standing over my left shoulder. He had obviously been counting the cards, looking for the right "index." I was on a $5 table and was betting a $5 progression. About the time I was making my first $50 bet, the young man laid down a $100 bill and told the dealer that "the money plays." The dealer received permission from the pit boss to accept cash for a bet and commenced to deal. The young man who I will refer to as Mr. Cool, looked just that. He must have figured that he had a massive advantage. The dealer gave me a 20 and Mr. Cool was forced to hit to a 13. The dealer had a 9 up. Mr. Cool busted and I won $50. The dealer had a 6 in the hole and drew to a bust. Out came another $100. Mr. Cook remained calm. I could see the contentment on his face as he received a two-card total of 20. The dealer's up card was a face card so I hit my 12 and stood on 19. The dealer's hole card was an ace. Needless to say, we lost. I now reverted back to the minimum bet. Mr. Cool pulled out another $100. Finally, a chance to get ahead! Mr. Cool received a pair of aces and split. The dealer's up card was a 7 and I had another 20. I could see that Mr. Cool was now getting nervous. In fact, he was starting to shake ever so slightly. The dealer delivered a 2 on one ace and a 5 on the other. I was prepared to catch Mr. Cool because his legs did not look very steady. The dealer had a 10 underneath and Mr. Cook was halfway out of the casino before I could look up to see his face. He probably went looking for the author whose advice he had followed! The moral to the story is, don't jump into a game with big bucks expecting to win just because the count is good. Make large bets only after a profit is assured. Mr. Cool needlessly lost $400 in about two minutes. He tried for the big kill and got it shoved up his tailpipe.

The $2 Progression

2-2-3-3-4-4-6-6-10-10-14-14-20-20

The minimum bet is $2 with a maximum of $20. All of the same rules apply to each progression. The only difference is the minimum and maximum bets to be made. The profits after losing the indicated number hand are as follows:

2nd = even • 3rd = $1 • 4th = $4 • 5th = $6 • 6th = $10 • 7th = $12 • 8th = $18 • 9th = $20 • 10th = $30 • 11th = $36 • 12th = $50 • 13th = $58 • 14th = $78 • Add $20 for each additional hand.

Nevada is currently one of the few gambling areas that still accepts bets less than $5. As other states legalize casino gambling, this will change. The $2 progression does not require much of a bankroll. A $100 bankroll will keep you in the game, even if the cards run "cold." After securing a $200 profit, I recommend going to the $5 progression for increased winnings.

One day in Reno, I decided to walk through a casino which was a shortcut to my car. I remembered that I still had two $1 chips that were to be used as tips for the waitresses. Since I was leaving, I decided to let the $2 ride on the blackjack table (friends were waiting for me at the car). I bet the $2 and won. Wouldn't you know it, these kinds of things always happen when you're in a hurry! I stayed with the $2 progression and walked out of the casino with an additional $100 after about ten minutes of play. I apologized to my friends for being late and offered to pay for lunch on the way home.

The $5 Progression

5-5-7-7-10-10-15-15-25-25-35-35-50-50

The profits after losing the indicated number hand are as follows: 2nd = even • 3rd = $3 • 4th = $10 • 5th = $14 • 6th = $24 • 7th = $29 • 8th = $44 • 9th = $49 • 10th = $74 • 11th = $89 • 12th = $124 • 13th = $144 • 14th = $194 • Add $50 for each additional hand.

I believe the $5 progression will be used by the majority of players who study this book. Most players can afford $5 tables if they use this progression. As stated earlier, you will not find tables for less than $5 in many gambling areas. Five dollar tables are always available during the day. In the evening they are hard to find in Atlantic City and the Bahamas. Casinos understand that the average player's bankroll cannot support a $10 minimum. They count on the players to take the risk (after all, it's the only game in town) and lose what money they have. This sounds cruel, and it is. The casinos know that the quickest way to lose money is to overbet one's bankroll. Do not let yourself be forced to bet over your head. Either have a large enough bankroll, or don't play when the table limits go up.

I have had a great deal of success with this progression. When my profits allow, I often jump into the $10 progression after winning the third $50 bet. In other words, I go to the first $70 bet of the $10 progression. Robin has often started with a $5 bet and reached double-down situations at the $100 level. We play the exact same strategy, but she always seems to have slightly more luck.

Robin and I recently flew down to the Bahamas on a gambling junket. We both played the $5 progression and did very well. On the plane down we noticed a young girl and her "Sugar Daddy." He was a rich, plump old geezer who really knew how to have a good time. At the casino he had a table to himself and played all seven positions. His girlfriend must have been off playing the slots. Robin and I felt like paupers next to this guy. He was wagering $200 on each of the seven spots. We were at a table adjacent to him betting a measly $5 progression. He was obviously not a counter or a progression player because he always made the same bet. We were all having a good time and making money. At one time I glanced over and noticed that he was at least $10,000 ahead! This wasn't all that hard to believe since he was betting $1,400 on each deal. Robin and I continued to plug on and moved to other tables when cards got cold. We were enjoying ourselves and forgot about the high roller. When the casino closed (which they do in the Bahamas) we were all driven back to board our plane. Robin and I were very satisfied with the performance of the progression system and wished we had used the $10 or $25 system.

After being seated on the plane we notice that "Sugar Daddy" was somewhat quiet and somber. I asked him how he had made out. He told us that he was at one time $20,000 ahead. He stated that he lost the $20,000 after his girlfriend joined him at the table. He claimed that she had brought him terrible luck. They did not appear to be speaking so I guess this guy really believed what he was saying. I could not understand how someone would allow himself to throw away twenty grand. It was easy to understand how he could lose it. After all, he always bet the same. One way or another, the house will win more hands! It was sad to hear that he had lost all that money, but it was obvious that he could afford it. Robin and I no longer felt like paupers. We were the ones who knew how to beat the casino!

The $25 Progression

25-25-35-35-50-50-75-75-125-125-175-175-250-250

The profits after losing the indicated number hand are as follows: 2nd = even • 3rd = $15 • 4th = $50 • 5th = $70 • 6th = $120 • 7th = $145 • 8th = $220 • 9th = $245 • 10th = $370 • 11th = $445 •

12th = $620 • 13th = $720 • 14th = $970 • Add $250 for each additional hand.

The $50 Progression

50-50-75-75-100-100-150-150-250-250-300-300-500-500

The profits after losing the indicated number hand are as follows: 2nd = even • 3rd = $25 • 4th = $100 • 5th = $150 • 6th = $250 • 7th = $300 • 8th = $450 • 9th = $500 • 10th = $750 • 11th = $900 • 12th = $1,250 • 13th = $1,450 • 14th = $1,950 • Add $500 for each additional hand.

The $100 Progression

100-100-150-150-200-200-300-300-500-500-700-700-1,000-1,000

The profits after losing the indicated number hand are as follows: 2nd = even • 3rd = $50 • 4th = $200 • 5th = $300 • 6th = $500 • 7th = $600 • 8th = $900 • 9th = $1,000 • 10th = $1,500 • 11th = $1,800 • 12th = $2,500 • 13th = $2,900 • 14th = $3,900 • Add $1,000 for each additional hand.

Can you imagine the money that "Sugar Daddy" could have won in the Bahamas if he had used this progression instead of betting $200 a hand!

You may build a progression based on any minimum value that you desire, as illustrated below, with X equal to the minimum bet:

$$X-X-3/2X-3/2X-2X-2X-3X-3X-5X-5X-7X-7X-10X-10X$$

Summary

There is no way to know when we are going to win or lose a hand of blackjack. The progression systems that I have introduced to you are the best means of ensuring that you win more money during "hot streaks" than you lose during "cold streaks." By keeping the minimum bet within the limitations of your bankroll you should survive runs of bad luck and ultimately beat the casino.

My progression system, coupled with "winning play strategy," will enable you to give the casino a run for its money as never before. Without such a system, how many of us could actually afford to make $100 bets?

I have taken the guesswork out of the game. A good player should not have to worry about his play or next bet. You will find progression betting easy to follow and will rapidly advance to higher bets. As your bankroll grows, so may your minimum bet. In the Money Management chapter I will discuss the recommended bankroll required for the various progression systems. It's about time that a good player, with average funds, has a shot at the big money!

Betting Progressions

$2
2-2-3-3-4-4-6-6-10-10-14-14-20-20

$5
5-5-7-7-10-10-15-15-25-25-35-35-50-50

$10
10-10-15-15-20-20-30-30-50-50-70-70-100-100

$25
25-25-35-35-50-50-75-75-125-125-175-175-250-250

$50
50-50-75-75-100-100-150-150-250-250-350-350-500-500

$100
100-100-150-150-200-200-300-300-500-500-700-700-1,000-1,000

Blackjack Skip Bet Rules

1. Upon receipt of 3/2 on a blackjack: skip one level of the progression.
2. Upon winning double or more on the bet: skip two levels unless the money you are risking is more than you just received.

5

Money Management

Every once in a while I find self-proclaimed professional gamblers pushing their wares on the cable channels. The segment is actually nothing more than a half-hour advertisement for various gambling videos. The show is similar to the "get rich in real estate" pitches that can be found in the wee hours of the morning.

It amazes me how these pitchmen can talk for half an hour without giving one piece of useful information. Of course, for $49.95 you will learn all you ever need to know!

Recently, one of the topics happened to be money management at the blackjack tables. The narrator discussed establishing "win goals." He defined "session money" as the money you have to play with during a round of play. It was stated that the win goal should be somewhere around 20 percent of the session money. In other words, if you go to the tables with $100 your win goal would be $20. He went on to explain that if you win the $20, pocket the original session money and half of the win goal money. Continue to play with the remaining $10 and quit if you lose it. This plan of attack assures the player of quitting ahead.

The win goal discussion was presented very well and appeared to make sense. But then I started asking the television screen the following questions: Now what do I do? Am I expected to win a measly $10 and go back and watch television in the hotel room? Do I wait an hour, day or month before I start a new session? If I'm not supposed to quit, what good is pocketing a $10 profit if I will be playing again in five minutes? I received no answers.

Most of the books I have read offer similar money management techniques. They all talk about such things as total bankroll, play bankroll and session money. Some advocate setting the win goal as high as 100% of the session money. In the previous example the player would have had a $100 win goal. Big deal!

The win goal strategy has some merit if the session money was $10,000. In that case, the win goal would be $2,000 and I would walk away with at least $1,000. Now we're talking about some decent money! But how many of us can afford $10,000 session money? I am convinced that these guys all design their money management systems based on unrealistic bankrolls.

The typical money management system requires that the minimum bet be somewhere between 1/150 to 1/1000 of the player's bankroll. This means that a minimum of $750 to $5,000 is required to play the $5 tables! By adhering to the minimum bet increment, the player is supposedly protected from losing the entire bankroll. Keep in mind that these money management systems were devised to support the card counting systems.

Many blackjack books contain charts that indicate the required bankroll, session money and betting "spreads." With the spread being the difference between the minimum and maximum bet the counter will make, based on the computed ratio or index. A book I recently read requires almost $2,000 to make $5 minimum bets and about $4,000 to make $10 bets. These requirements alone are enough to convince players not to mess with counting systems. If that kind of money is required to support counters, the system must have serious flaws!

I strongly believe in simplification. I do not feel it is necessary to come up with intricate charts and special terminology to make a system appear more scientific. It's cut and dried. The money you take with you on a gambling trip is your bankroll. If you plan on staying two days, then risk only half of it the first day. Common sense tells us not to lose all the money the first day unless you like the idea of sitting in your room broke. As far as session money goes, that's up to you. You know how much you can possibly lose in one day, so you divide it up into parts. If you want to visit five different casinos that day, divide the money so you can have a session at each casino. We are not children, we can figure this stuff out!

A more realistic win goal is to take home as much money as you can! Players, as a whole, do not get to gamble very often. I'm not going to stop because I have won some predetermined number of dollars, and I don't think you will either. Does it make sense to fly from Florida to Vegas only to quit gambling after two hours because I got hot? Get real! Gamblers go to the tables to make money and enjoy themselves. Of course, if I have a losing streak I will get up from the tables and do something else for a while. My point is that the various systems on the market are a bunch of fluff, statistics, charts and useless words. They do not take into account the reason people gamble, or the money they actually have to risk.

One reason that count systems require so much money is to allow for the spread. This spread usually ranges from two to five times the original bet, depending on the system and bankroll available. The recommended spread is actually quite small when the bankroll is less than $1,000. This smaller spread reduces the effectiveness of the counting systems which again puts the average gambler at a disadvantage.

My betting progression minimum bet is based on bankroll size. The maximum bet is not! I do not cringe at losing large bets. In fact, the larger the bet I lose, the more money I'm ahead. Progression betting does not require thousands of dollars in order to make large bets, as with the count systems. The available bankroll determines the maximum progression I can afford. The number of hands I win in a row determines the maximum bet.

TABLE 5.1

RECOMMENDED BLACKJACK BANKROLLS

Minimum Bet	Minimum Bankroll
$2	$100
$5	$250
$10	$500
$25	$1,250
$50	$2,500
$100	$5,000

The bankroll obviously changes as you win or lose. If playing the $5 progression ($250 minimum) and you win $250, you may shift to the $10 progression. On the other hand, if losing, there is nothing wrong with dropping to a lower progression. This strategy will keep you in the chips during a long dry spell.

I make no attempt to dream up a session loss limit. Use good judgment and move to another table if you're having bad luck. I usually move to another table if I lose 3 or 4 hands in a row. I also move if I lose money on the shoe. You will be surprised at how luck can vary from one table to another. If changing tables isn't the solution, I often walk to another casino. Obviously, this is hard to do on a cruise ship or in Freeport!

As I have explained, the idea of a win limit is idiotic. This does not mean that I am willing to let the casino win back my profits! I closely monitor my winnings and move if I'm on the decline. I may quit for a while when luck is real bad.

Never quit in the middle of a hot streak! Always wait until the cards cool off. Take advantage of a good table and ride it for all it is worth.

Make sure that the progression you choose is in line with your bankroll. In Atlantic City don't expect to find a table under $10 in the evening. Keep in mind that the minimum bankroll is for one player, playing one hand. If your spouse is playing, you should each have the minimum bankroll.

Do not let the status of the bankroll determine play. If you have a split or double-down situation, do it! The play strategy must never be altered. Only too often I have observed players becoming gun-shy and fail to double because their bankroll was low. If you can't stand the heat, get out of the casino!

Summary

Money management should not be a complicated evolution. All that is needed is a sufficient bankroll to support the chosen progression. Keep winning as long as you can. Divide the bankroll by the number of days you plan on playing. Determine how many sessions per day you desire and proportion the money accordingly. Don't hesitate to move to another table/casino if you're having bad luck. Set your own guidelines for when to move and stick to them. Always be prepared to lose, but with my system, expect to win! Most of all, have a great time. After all, you only live once.

6

Home Improvement

You now have the tools necessary to play winning blackjack. You have read and understand the play strategy and are familiar with the betting progressions. It's time to rush out to the casino, right? Wrong! As with all newly acquired skills, one must practice to become proficient. Winning blackjack demands a reflex decision process. There is no room for intuition, guesswork or indecision. The player must know exactly what actions to take under all situations.

Reading this book is only the first step toward becoming a successful player. You must now "learn" the strategy presented through practice and play at home. Risking your hard earned money at the casino tables is not recommended until you are able to make all the correct plays and bet decisions with no hesitation. There isn't time to refer to notes or crib sheets once you sit down at a blackjack table. You either know what you are doing or you don't.

By following the practice suggestions made in this chapter, your "homework" can be made more interesting and downright entertaining. The time required to acquire adequate skill is entirely up to you. Some players may require several practice sessions and others may gain proficiency in only one session. Luckily for all of us, the strategy that I have presented is logical and quite simple. Unlike card counters, you are not required to become math experts or memorize mazes of charts.

The key to making the most out of your practice sessions is to establish the most realistic conditions possible. In other words, ensure that the "house rules" coincide with the actual rules you will encounter at the casino. For your convenience, the basic guidelines are as follows:

1. Dealer must hit to hard 17 or more.
2. Player may only double on 10 or 11.
3. Aces may only be split once.
4. Only one card is dealt to a split ace.
5. Player receives 3/2 for a natural.
6. Player receives 2/1 insurance.
7. A minimum of four decks of cards should be used.

If you know for sure that the casino you plan on going to allows more liberal rules, play with their rules. Otherwise, follow the guidelines as listed.

A home computer with a good blackjack program is the most convenient way to practice. If this method is used, ensure that the program is realistic and allows you to make all of the progression bets in the sequence. (Some programs only allow even numbered money bets, for example.)

Although most casinos use six to eight decks of cards, I recommend four decks for convenience's sake. More than four decks gets cumbersome and takes too long to shuffle. It is not necessary to use a shoe; cut the cards as described in Chapter 1 and remember to burn the first card.

You may play the game solitary fashion, but I recommend playing with spouse and/or friend(s). Rotate the deal occasionally to give the dealer a break. When a dealer gets too hot, it's also a good time to switch dealers!

It doesn't matter how many hands are dealt; however, each should be treated separately. They should each be supported by a separate bankroll and follow the bet progression. For this reason I do not recommend dealing out more than two hands if playing alone. It becomes too difficult to keep track of each hand's bet status.

Chips or coins may be used. I have found that keeping a running total on a hand-held calculator to be the easiest way to track the bankroll. This requires a calculator for each hand but it sure beats shifting chips back and forth.

In the beginning, use the $10 progression strictly for convenience. Start with $500 in chips or on the calculator and watch it grow. Play only one hand per person and have the play strategy and betting charts in front of you. Refer to the tables for every play decision and to determine the next bet. Do not forget to make the appropriate jump bet after blackjacks, splits and double downs.

After becoming familiar with the tables, only look at them when in doubt. When the tables are no longer required, you are ready to take on the casinos! By this time, all play and betting becomes a reflex action.

In addition to learning, the practice sessions should build up your confidence in my play strategy and betting progressions. If you don't find better results than with any "system" you've tried before, I would be very surprised. The betting progressions that I have developed have exceeded all of my expectations.

7

The Card Counter Challenge

Today's blackjack authors/experts who continue to sugarcoat the card-counting strategy are not giving the public an even shake. On the surface, these strategies appear to be sure winners. The reality is, they are not.

As stated earlier, at one time counters held a significant advantage over the casinos, but with the introduction of multiple decks, quick shuffles and numerous rule changes those days no longer exist. Although a "professional" can still earn money using the count, a large bankroll is required to support the effort. The advantages seen today are nowhere close to those of the early 1960s.

What boils my blood is that today's so-called experts must know that the average recreational player does not have the capital required, or the time, to support the counting systems. Yet, they continue to write and sell books and videos to the average John Doe. Don't get me wrong, the authors I refer to are not crooks or con men. Their teachings are based on a sound mathematical foundation. They merely fail to stress the weakness of the count and the capital required.

I feel sorry for the poor soul whose charter bus arrives in Atlantic City at 9 PM on a Saturday night. He possesses a $200 bankroll, has memorized a typical count strategy, and expects to board the bus at 6 AM with big bucks. In all probability, with only $10 minimum tables available, the guy won't survive more than an hour. He will spend one of the longest nights of his life waiting for that bus. I know. I also followed the advice of many a self-proclaimed expert!

I challenge any and all "published" blackjack authors who teach card counting to prove their systems! I will play head to head, but insist on playing with a bankroll that the average player would be willing to lose, and under the play conditions he or she would most likely encounter.

I have no argument with the play strategy the counters teach; all are based on sound strategy. My intent is to prove that the betting strategies and money management systems taught are not realistic and do not hold up under today's game.

To accurately compare our betting systems and money management, I insist that the following conditions be established:

1. We use a $300 maximum bankroll.
2. We play from a shoe with a minimum of six decks.
3. We play with a table minimum of $5.
4. We base all bets on the strategy in our books. In other words, we practice what we preach!
5. We will play the same hands! The only difference will be the amount of money wagered. I will agree to use their play strategy or mine. The intent is to compare betting and money management strategies. By playing "duplicate blackjack" there will be no doubt as to which betting strategy is superior.
6. We will play a minimum of ten shoes or until one of us loses our bankroll.

I feel very confident in the preceding challenge. Requirements 1 through 3 were established to ensure we play under the conditions a typical player will most likely encounter. Requirements 4 and 5 ensure that the betting systems we teach are put to the test.

The irony of the challenge is that most counting systems taught are not even eligible for the challenge! Although requirements 1 through 3 are typical conditions an average player encounters, the counting systems cannot meet these requirements. Most of the "experts" require a minimum bankroll of approximately $1,000 to play a $5 table. Under condition number 4, bets must be based on the strategies taught in our books. Therefore, most count systems cannot be used under the most typical of conditions!

I could not think of a better way to point out the inadequacies of the count systems taught today. They cannot be used with a $300 bankroll on a $5 table! The average blackjack player is willing to risk between $200 to $500. No casinos in Atlantic City, the Bahamas or cruise ships offer blackjack tables with less than a $5 minimum. Most tables in Nevada have a $5 or more limit. This tells me that the majority of the "count" authors are telling us that the average person should never play blackjack! Then why in the hell do they sell us the books and videos!

I doubt there will be any takers on my challenge. If there are, I am sure that the progression betting system will prevail. I have spent more time than I wish to remember comparing the strategies. The "card counter challenge" is the best way for you the reader to make your own comparison. Follow the conditions as I have stated (four decks is okay) and see for yourself which strategy is superior.

Summary

The card counter challenge presented in this chapter was originally intended to give me the opportunity to take on the "big boys." It wasn't until I began to develop this chapter that I realized that the majority of the "counting" systems were not even eligible to compete. I immediately realized that I had stumbled onto the biggest drawback to the count strategy. It does not apply to 99 percent of today's blackjack players!

For years I tried various "count" systems. Every time they failed to return expected profits. I chalked it up to bad luck—after all, the count must work! It took me several years to realize that the count was overblown and dependent on a large bankroll. Once introduced to the theory of positive progression, my luck changed. As I developed my own progression I was able to understand why the count had been such a letdown.

To this day, I cannot understand why the count system is still held in such high regard. The casinos are not stupid; they were able to significantly reduce the advantage of the count. Yet today, the public is taught that the count is the only way to beat the house. I can understand how Columbus must have felt when he tried to convince everyone that the world was round!

The misconception of the count is further emphasized by Hollywood. In the movie *Rain Man* the charactor played by Dustin Hoffman was able to take the casino for a bundle through his ability to remember what cards had been played. I loved the movie, but as a blackjack player I thought this particular scene was ridiculous. Large bets were made and won, based on seeing a few cards from a six- or eight-deck shoe. It left the impression that card counting is a sure thing. Why didn't the dealer get the 20's and blackjacks? I am also capable of determining the exact count at any point in an eight-deck shoe. Why haven't I ever won that kind of money! If there was a system developed that gave the advantage portrayed in *Rain Man*, I would be sitting at the tables instead of in front of this word processor.

I make no claim to being a blackjack expert. I have never made my living at the tables and have no desire to do so in the future. I play blackjack mostly for recreation and am successful through the betting progressions. I am willing to bet that very few self-proclaimed experts have ever, or are, currently making a living playing the game. As with all games of chance, blackjack is a gamble. If you want a sure thing, do not enter a gambling casino.

Learn the strategies and betting progressions in this book, then practice until you're proficient. Compare the strategies presented with those of your favorite card counter. Upon completion of the card counting challenge, I am confident that you will rethink the card counting strategy, as I have.

8

Blackjack "Past"

One form or another of gambling has existed on earth for uncountable millenia. In no known time period or culture has it not been a part of human life. The *Academic American Encyclopedia* records that dice carved from the ankle bones of antelope were discovered in prehistoric tombs and burial caves. Other gambling implements have been found among artifacts of ancient China, India and Egypt. The *Encyclopedia of America* documents evidence that ivory dice dating before 1500 BC were found at Thebes and that gambling was mentioned on a still older tablet found in the Pyramid of Cheops in Egypt. I can just picture a prehistoric ancestor of Jimmy the Greek blowing on the dice and chanting "Come on seven, baby needs a new pair of shoes!"

Playing cards are believed to have originated in the Orient. It is documented that the French utilized them as early as the fourteenth century. The deck of cards as we know it today (consisting of four distinct suits), is said to have evolved from Tarot cards, which may account for the many who believe that fortunes can be made at the blackjack tables. (Sorry about that!).

Despite the longevity of gambling, the practice was generally considered vulgar and was illegal in the United States until relatively recently. The first United States Blue Law regulating gambling was passed in 1624 by the Virginia Assembly. The law stated that "Mynisters shall not give themselves to excess in drinking or yette spend their tyme idelie by day or night, playing at dice, cards or any unlawful game." The first gambling legislation passed March 22, 1630, in Boston, Massachusetts. The legislation read, "It is ordered that all persons whatsoever that have cards, dice or tables in their houses, shall make away with them before the next court under pain of punishment." It makes you wonder where the family was expected to eat their dinner!

Historians document that casino gambling in the United States was rampant yet illegal. It can easily be equated to the consumption of alcohol during the Prohibition years. Thanks to modern progress (and a little shove from Organized Crime), casino gambling was legalized in Nevada in 1931. Atlantic City (New Jersey) was to follow suit and legalized casino gambling in 1978.

The specific origin of twenty-one (blackjack) is somewhat clouded. The French and Italians both lay claim to the game. It is most generally accepted that blackjack originated in French casinos about the year 1700. The Italians claim that blackjack evolved from a similar game of theirs called "seven and a half." The fact that the American Hoyle of 1875 called blackjack *vingt un* and that Foster's Hoyle in the 1800s called the game *vingt-et-un* (French for twenty-one) lends credence to the French claims. It also explains why many English and some Americans refer to blackjack as "van john" or "pontoon" which is Texan slang for *vingt-et-un*.

There is not documentation (that I am aware of) that confirms or refutes that blackjack was played in the saloons of the Wild West. It's hard to imagine Doc Holliday or Billy the Kid saying to the dealer, "Hit me!" Poker, roulette and faro (described in the glossary) are depicted as the games of choice, a fact which no fan of a good western would argue. The fact of the matter is, there were very few gambling saloons and only a handful of shootouts during that entire period of American history. The abundance of gambling halls and shootouts makes far more entertaining reading and viewing than reality. After all, what would *High Noon* have been without the climactic gunfight!

For simplicity's sake, and to prevent this from becoming just another boring history lesson, we will consider the legalization of casino gambling in Nevada (1931) as the origin of American casino blackjack. Blackjack started out low on the popularity scale. It was surpassed by craps, roulette and faro. The common belief was that blackjack could not be beat since players were required to "hit" prior to the dealer. As long as the dealer was able to collect "bust" money without having to chance a bust, the game was considered too risky. As with most games of chance, good players evolved and discovered ways to slice into the casino's advantage.

Another significant concern the early players had was the numerous ways and ease in which a player could be cheated at blackjack. It is common knowledge that gangsters and mobsters were behind many of the early casinos. Despite the casinos' legal and natural advantage several houses were not beyond cheating in order to up the profits. Dr. Edward O. Thorp points out (in *Beat the Dealer*) that he was informed that in the first five years of the Nevada Gaming Control Board's operation, more than twenty casinos were closed down for cheating. Among the methods used were "peeking," "dealing seconds," "marking cards," "deck stacking" and the use of "mechanics." By peeking at the top card the dealer decided whether to receive it or to deal himself the next card (deal a second). If the dealer had a total of thirteen and the top card was a ten, you could be sure that the dealer would receive the next card hoping for an eight or less. There was obviously no guarantee that the "second" would help, but it was better than a sure bust with the top card. The dealers were extremely skilled and could rarely be detected peeking or dealing the second. If caught, it was merely a matter of a "poor loser's" word against that of an honorable dealer! Marking the back of the cards was another method the dealer had to determine the need to deal a second. This method was advantageous because it eliminated the need to peek, but was risky in that it produced physical evidence that could be used to prosecute the dealer/casino. Skilled dealers also cheated by stacking the deck. By picking up the cards and shuffling in certain ways the dealers were able to stack the deck to the house's advantage. This was feasible, particularly since all games were dealt using a single deck. The customary practice of the dealer piking up the used cards and placing them face up at the bottom of the (unused) deck was another vehicle to cheat the players. The talented dealer could easily use any one of the discards to bust a player or improve his or her hand. Another of the crooked casinos methods to boost blackjack profits was the use of mechanics. These were the "Cy Youngs" (one of baseball's greatest pitchers) of dealers. They were put into the game when it was desired to fleece the players having huge bankrolls or win back large sums from a lucky winner. These mechanics were top of the line and could peek, deal seconds, and stack the deck with the best of them.

Not all cheating was on behalf of the casino. Dishonest dealers were known to use the techniques described to deal their friends or partners winning hands in order to share the "pie." These dealers had to be especially talented and careful to avoid detection by the casino. If caught, they were likely to wind up pushing up daisies under a goal post. To cover the house losses to their partner, these dealers would merely have to take more money from the rest of the players at the table.

All good things must come to an end. The public became very aware of the various cheating techniques and pressure was applied to clean up the game. The Gaming Commission became more involved and the incidents of cheating declined. Government investigations, as well as printed articles exposing cheating appearing in such well-known magazines as *Life*, were prime catalysts in cleaning up the Nevada gaming industry.

One of the first and most famous published experts on blackjack was a man named John Scarne. He was recognized as the world's foremost authority on games of chance. During World War II, as gaming advisor to the United States Armed Forces, his job was to give lectures and demonstrations to help prevent the troops from being cheated overseas. You can bet that he had a good handle on the cheating techniques discussed in the previous paragraphs. He was consulted by the United States Senate, the Federal Bureau of Investigation, the British Home Office, and Puerto Rican Government, Panama—the list goes on. He also served as game consultant to the *Encyclopedia Britannica* and the *World Book Encyclopedia*, and wrote several books, notably *Scarne's Complete Guide to Gambling*.

In 1957 John Scarne served as gaming consultant to the Havana Hilton Hotel Casino in Cuba. He claimed credit for introducing the four-deck blackjack dealing box (shoe) and the procedure to deal all player's cards face-up during this period. He also advised the casino not to put into play the last 40 percent or more of the bottom cards. Thus, the cut "indicator card" was born. These changes to the game are of major significance. Until then all blackjack games used a single deck and all of the cards were usually played. Scarne's suggestion of using a shoe eliminated 95 percent of the cheating methods used by dealers and players. Dealing the players' cards up helped players to count but prevented them from marking or switching cards. Use of the indicator card and not playing the last 40 percent of the cards virtually eliminated "end play." The good news is, these changes did not immediately take place in the United States.

A handful of blackjack experts in the United States had developed their own counting systems similar to those discussed in the Systems chapter. These players were becoming quite successful. End play created situations where large profits could be made with absolutely no risk. Why John Scarne's recommendations in Cuba did not immediately carry over to the United States is beyond me! Scarne's Havana Hilton recommendations were not introduced in Nevada for several years. *Scarne's Complete Guide to Gambling*, published in 1961, introduced the public to card counting. Even though his publication resulted in some Nevada rule changes, he did not receive the attention or credit that Dr. Edward O. Thorp was about to receive. One has to believe that the mention of Dr. Thorp left a bad taste in Scarne's mouth.

It was interesting to note John Scarne's assertion that he was the first player to beat blackjack using a count system and in 1947 was the first of those to be barred from the casinos in Las Vegas. He explains that he was barred because he told Benjamin ("Bugsy") Siegel, builder of the Flamingo Hotel Casino, that he could beat them with a countdown, was challenged, and beat them. He goes on to explain that he was barred at casinos throughout Nevada and the rest of the country. This story indicates to me that Scarne had one hell of an ego, had a lapse in good judgment, or, the event took place in his dreams. What impact John Scarne really had on today's game is hard to say. There are many who claim to be the first to use a count system. In fact, Dr. Edward O. Thorp credits a man named Benjamin F. Smith with using the first successful count system. The more one digs into it the more confusing it gets. Almost every author to date credits different people for reducing the casino's advantage. About the only exception is John Scarne who claimed to be the first to change the game, use the count, and who got barred and caused Nevada rules to be changed! Ironically, he is rarely, if ever, mentioned by the majority of the blackjack authors. If everything he stated is accurate, he deserves recognition. I do find it hard to believe that if the Nevada casinos were aware that a count system could beat them as early as 1947, they would wait until the 1960s to change the rules of the game. You must believe that the casinos are no dummies. When they discover a significant player advantage in any game they take quick action to counteract the advantage! I must give John Scarne credit for at least one thing—he is the first of a long line of self-proclaimed experts to proudly claim banishment from casinos. For some, it serves as good publicity for their system and gives them an excuse for not having to put the system to practice. As we all know, the philosophy of "do as I say, not as I do" has become far too easy to live by. I have always been leery of gentlemen who want me to pay them to learn their money-making system!

Before we go any further, I should discuss some of the liberal rules that existed prior to the many rule changes that occurred in the 1960s and 1970s. The game of blackjack was a true bonanza for a few players with adequate financial backing and the ability to case the deck. The house dealt from a single deck, all cards were dealt face down except for the dealer's last card. Most importantly, on most occasions, every card in the deck was put into play. This fact alone allowed a counter to know exactly what cards remained at the end of the deck! To add icing to the cake, the players were allowed to double-down on any two cards, split aces repeatedly, and take as many cards on split aces as desired. It's no wonder that casino blackjack rapidly rose to become one of the most popular games. In some casinos, players were even given a bonus if they received an actual "black" jack with an ace (beyond the standard 3/2). Bonuses or automatic wins were also offered for a player drawing more than a specified number of cards (without busting). Many casinos allowed the players the option to "surrender." This rule allowed the player to throw in the towel after receiving the first two cards. The player essentially acknowledged likely defeat and paid the house half of the initial wager in lieu of continuing play with the two cards dealt. In the long run surrender was a money-saving proposition for the players. With a two-card total of fifteen or sixteen it was a wise decision to surrender against the dealer's 10-value card (particularly if the remaining deck is known to be rich in high value cards). With a sound play strategy, adequate bankroll, and a decent count system, the game was ripe for the picking. To compound the casino's heartache with counters, dealers had to put up with cheats who would find ways to mark the cards or switch them. Players were allowed to handle the cards and were directed to scrape the table surface when a hit was desired. This created a temptation that was too hard for some to ignore.

Overall, the casinos were still raking in large profits at the blackjack tables. Only a small group of people were able to take full advantage of the liberal rules. The average player did not really understand the game, nor was he financially equipped to be a threat to the casino if he did. There was yet to be a consensus on proper play strategy nor was a powerful counting system in use.

Discussing the development of basic play strategy is not quite as foggy as trying to determine who the first card counter really was. Four mathematicians in the United States Army are believed to be the first to develop calculations which would significantly reduce the house advantage. They were Herbert Maisel, Roger R. Baldwin, James P. McDermott and Wilbur E. Cantey. Their work was published in the *Journal of the American Statistical Association* in 1956. Dr. Edward O. Thorp is credited with being the first to use an IBM 704 computer to improve upon the aforementioned strategy. Finally, Julian H. Braun of IBM refined Dr. Thorp's calculations to actually give a good player a slight advantage over the casino. Mr. Braun is credited with having the most widely followed calculations. Every play strategy taught today is based upon his findings.

What the consensus can agree on is that Dr. Edward O. Thorp, professor of Mathematics at the University of California, put an accurate play strategy together with a very strong 10-count system (and later an even stronger point-count system) and completely changed the future of blackjack! Dr. Thorp published *Beat the Dealer* in 1962 and has been considered the most significant authority ever since. At last, millions of blackjack players were exposed to a strategy and system that could put the casino on the losing end of the deal. Dr. Thorp's book received worldwide attention. He became a celebrity almost overnight and became the primary candidate for the Gambler's Hall of Fame (if one were to exist). Card counters came from everywhere, armed with Dr.

Thorp's system. The casinos could no longer conduct business as usual. You better believe that the casino owners called in the brightest minds they could find to reestablish their advantage over the player.

The obvious defenses were to shuffle the cards more often and to eliminate end play. Dealers were taught count systems and were trained to shuffle when the count shifted to the player's advantage. They were also instructed to shuffle when large increases in bets were made. In addition, aces could no longer be split more than once and only one card could be received on a split ace. On April 1, 1964, the Las Vegas Resort Hotel Association announced that two more major rules of blackjack were being changed. This time the casinos forbade the splitting of aces and only allowed the player to double-down on hard 11 only. These particular changes backfired on the casinos and created a loss in revenue due to a decline in play. Players were angry over the drastic rule changes and stayed away from the tables. Dealers were upset and raised hell because of the substantial loss in tips. Within a few weeks the casinos caved into the pressure and abandoned these two rule changes.

Being of sound mind, the casinos found more subtle ways to reduce the counter's advantage. Multiple-deck shoes were employed which completely devastated the card counting systems for several reasons. By introducing multiple decks the casinos were able to reduce the percentage of cards seen by the players and by way of a new cutting procedure and use of the plastic indicating card. The combination of more cards and a large percent of unseen cards effectively reduced the significance of the running count (index number) to a useless statistic. With multiple decks, the running count rarely identifies advantageous situations. In no way does it ever give the player with an average size bankroll the green light to make a large bet. Most importantly, the introduction of multiple decks completely did away with end play. As stressed many times over, end play was the most significant advantage that the early card counter had. Ironically, the greatest defense that the casino could employ was given to the Havana Hilton Hotel Casino in 1957 by a card counter named John Scarne!

The casinos eventually terminated the player's ability to double-down on any two cards and allowed them to double-down on a ten or eleven only. The surrender option was removed as well as the bonus payoffs discussed earlier. Many of the blackjack rule changes were enacted because of the new strategy statistics developed by Dr. Thorp and Mr. Braun, and they had very little to do with card counting.

Many of the casinos in Nevada also switched to dealing all of the players' cards up. This tactic made it much easier for card counters to count but prevented the players from touching the cards. It is quite obvious that the casinos do not fear the counters. Otherwise, why would they make the count easier by dealing the cards up!

The casino's blackjack game was temporarily threatened by computer-generated strategies and Dr. Thorp's 10-count and point-count systems. As one would expect, casino management responded with more than enough defense mechanisms to overcome the threat. In fact, the casinos owe Dr. Thorp a great deal of thanks for the increased revenues and business he has encouraged their way through the years. The gaming industry wants the public to believe that their games can be beat! The casinos love to see new faces pop up with exciting new techniques to beat them. Every time a blackjack guru holds a seminar or advertises his wares on television, he is drumming up more interest and business for the casinos. The casinos have seen it all and are not afraid of counters.

In 1963 a professional gambler and pit boss for one of the largest casinos in Las Vegas published a book titled *How to Win*. Unfortunately for me, and millions of others, I was unaware of the book until I came across a reprint in the 1970s. As with the rest of the blackjack enthusiasts, I was absorbed in the card counting frenzy. *How to Win* was a casino insider's viewpoint on all aspects of casino gambling. Mr. Goodman made it extremely clear that no system to date was worth the paper on which it was printed. He emphasized that the primary reason most players lost is because they rarely have a basic understanding of the game. His contention was that accurate knowledge of the game (play strategy) coupled with proper money management could make the house vulnerable. *How to Win* was not specifically a blackjack book. It also covered horse racing, poker, roulette, craps and related subjects. I probably overlooked the book because it was not specific to blackjack and in the 1960s I would have scoffed at any author who did not advocate card counting.

Mike Goodman made no bones about it; casinos did not fear system players. He recognized that card counting was no match for the gaming industry. He rarely, if ever, referred specifically to counting but grouped card casers as "system players." His contention was that systems were inadequate in that they did not ensure that larger bets were made when on a winning streak. (Note: this is my interpretation of his writing.) Most significantly, he presented a betting progression that did ensure that larger bets would be made when on a "hot streak." *How to Win*'s approach to casino games, and more specifically blackjack, was almost too simple to believe.

Mr. Goodman's book has probably had little impact on the gaming industry. He has never received the publicity or admiration that John Scarne or Dr. Edward O. Thorp have received. Ironically, Mike Goodman made a personal challenge to Dr. Thorp and Mr. Scarne, as well as others, to test their systems at his casino or to a one-on-one debate. As of this writing (almost 30 years later!), there have been no takers of which I am aware.

In the 1970s, after losing faith in card counting, I became desperate and was in search of a better way. I discovered *How to Win*, and my approach to the game has not been the same since. In addition to an improved win-to-loss ratio over card counting, Mr. Goodman's progression allowed me to feel like a high roller for the first time in my life! I have sat next to thousands of counters over the years but have yet to see any of them get the attention from the pit boss that I have received as a progression player. I received the greatest kick observing my wife Robin on a "roll." I liked to sit back and watch as she progressed from a $5 to $100 bet in a matter of minutes. I could often see the pit bosses giving occasional glances in the beginning of the streak, followed by intense stares as she progressed. Although Robin is a beautiful woman, and has caught many a man's eye, it was not her looks that was getting the attention! These guys were trying to figure out what system she was using. They were very interested in trying to determine what the next bet would be after winning a double-down for $200. I imagine they were slightly intrigued with how calm she remained making such large bets. After all, she started out as a $5 bettor! When the streak did come to an end, they were most likely impressed with the willpower she had in order to drop back to a measly $5 bet again. I'm sure the management had seen similar techniques one time or another. By their expressions, I believe they were seeing the best! I had many similar experiences but was too busy watching the cards and the dealer to notice the pit boss's. I can tell you that we were often asked to fill in little cards with our names, address, occupation, etc. We were treated with a great deal of respect and often offered meals and other such "comps."

From personal observation and experience, I have never seen the casinos flinch when a counter (including myself) was at the table. The greatest concern shown was during hot streaks with the progression. As I think about it, I would also be concerned. A progression bettor always bets small when the cards are cold and always bets large when the cards are hot. The casino will never win much from a progression bettor but may lose a great deal. The greatest aspect of the progression system is that the casinos have no defense against it. They can shuffle all they want and it won't bother me! They can deal from a twelve-deck shoe and it still won't bother me!

Through the years, the gaming world has come to the conclusion that cheating the players is not worth the risk. The only cheating that might take place is by a dishonest dealer trying to pad his or her pockets. The casino management monitors every game very closely and is always on the alert for a crooked dealer. Taking the cards out of the hands of the dealers (with the shoe) and not allowing patrons to touch the cards, has virtually eliminated all cheating from either side of the table. There has continued to be a lot of talk about casinos still cheating. This talk is more than likely the sour grapes spewing forth from poor losers. Many of the self-professed experts often discuss being cheated as a crutch for failure of their system to perform up to their claims. In over twenty years at the tables, I cannot recall a single time that I even thought that cheating may have occurred. I have witnessed many a poor loser falsely accuse a lucky dealer, however.

Business boomed at the gaming tables through the mid-sixties and seventies. Much of this can be attributed to the hundreds of books and videos released during those years. Over the years, many of the Nevada casinos have returned to the more liberal blackjack rules and have offered some interesting variations of the game. Double- and single-deck games are scarce but can be found. Dealers at the double- and single-deck games are very well equipped to cope with card counters. Rules allowing players to double-down on any two cards have also resurfaced. The state of Nevada has given the casinos a great deal of leeway to control the games as they please. This has kept the players returning to Nevada and has created competition among the casinos to lure the players. One interesting variation of blackjack that has been offered is to let the players see both of the dealer's cards! The only drawback is that all "pushes" go to the casino. At first it sounds like a real deal for the player, but in actuality it is to the house's advantage. Oh, damn!

Atlantic City, New Jersey, joined Nevada by legalizing casino gambling in 1978. The residents of Atlantic City saw this as a way to save the city through increased revenues. The legalization of gambling did create more jobs but has yet to do much for the city. Reno and Las Vegas are exciting and relatively clean cities. Excitement and glamour are everywhere. Atlantic City, on the other hand, reminds me of one big slum with a few nice-looking casinos. The Atlantic City boardwalk is usually crowded with derelicts and pickpockets. The last time I dared to walk the boardwalk two separate attempts were made to lift my wallet. I only wish I could say they failed because the wallet was too fat.

As the casinos in Atlantic City have failed to rebuild the city, they have also failed to provide adequate gambling facilities for us common folk. The minimum table limits have been too high from day one. During a weekend or holiday a player is literally forced to play at a $10 or $25 table. One New Year's Eve the lowest minimum-bet table Robin and I could find open was $25. We saw hundreds of poor souls milling around hoping to find a $5 table, which did not exist. The state has always had very strict control over the Atlantic City casinos. All games must be dealt from a shoe and must consist of six or eight decks. There are no variations of the rules from one casino to another. Double-downs are only allowed on a ten or eleven. When Atlantic City first opened its casinos in 1978 "surrender" was offered. In 1982 the casinos terminated the option. To put it bluntly, compared to gambling in Nevada, Atlantic City sucks!

During the early years of Atlantic City casinos a card counter named Ken Uston came to fame after being banned from the casinos for counting. He has written a few books on blackjack and is another among a long line of self-professed experts. The story goes that he and a few partners were banned from Resorts International after taking them for over a hundred thousand in about a week's time. He filed a lawsuit and became famous. His story even made

CBS's *60 Minutes*. In 1982 the New Jersey Supreme Court decided against the casinos and told them they could not exclude suspected card counters unless the New Jersey Casino Control Commission authorized such regulation. As you might expect, the Casino Control Commission never has done so to date. Let's face it, everybody won! Mr. Uston gained credibility and probably sold tons of books due to the publicity. The Atlantic City casinos received the publicity that they badly needed and drew in thousands of new counters looking for that pot of gold! I get a real kick from all the talk about banishment. It is like a Medal of Honor to a counter to be banned from a casino. There isn't one count system author who doesn't touch on the subject and discuss how to avoid detection as a counter. They usually brag about the many times they were ejected and how they were forced to return in disguise. The casinos absolutely love it! Let the suckers who buy those books and videos believe the system is so powerful that the dealers will shake in their boots when they walk in! This is exactly the perception the casinos want people to have. Sure, some counters have been banned, non-counters have been as well. If I ran a casino and someone was "hot" or had an unbelievable streak of luck, I would most certainly consider asking them to leave. In many cases, I can't help but believe that banning card counters is all part of a plot to keep the card counting myth alive. As long as the public feels that the game of blackjack can easily be beat by counting, they will continue to flock to the blackjack tables en masse. They will also continue to buy the hundreds of card counting books and videos available.

From the time when casino gambling was legalized in Nevada to the present, only a handful of individuals have had significant impact on the game of blackjack. I include among this handful John Scarne, Dr. Edward O. Thorp, and Julian Braun. Almost every strategy and counting system published since has been nothing more than a rehash of their contributions. The problem is, the early works of Dr. Thorp and John Scarne were written to defeat the blackjack game as it was prior to 1962, yet authors continue to milk counting systems that were only applicable then. I fell victim to the card counting myth myself and helped line the pockets of many a blackjack guru. I believed in the count and stuck with it for over ten years. As with millions of others, I began to look elsewhere.

Luckily, I discovered *How to Win* by Mike Goodman. Not very many were as lucky as I was. They either quit playing blackjack altogether or decided to keep losing with the count systems. I have grown to develop a sincere distaste for many of the so-called experts whose mission seems to be to send their readers to the slaughter. They resemble many of those greasy vultures that may be found on late-night television selling get-rich schemes for hundreds and even thousands of dollars. Some poor souls send in their life savings for a shot at the good life. One con artist gets thousands of dollars from people to attend his real estate seminars and even encourages them to mortgage their homes, if necessary, in order to come up with the tuition fee! As it turns out, less than ten percent of those involved break even, yet this guy goes on legally making millions while completely destroying people's lives. Obviously, blackjack gurus are not in the same league, but the principle is the same.

9

Blackjack "Present and Future"

Gambling is currently the leading industry in the United States. It brings in well over $500 billion annually, much of which is illegal. Practically everyone has the "itch" to participate at one time or another. Among gamblers, card playing is the number one activity. It is difficult to determine the number of blackjack players, but one would expect it to be in the millions, and climbing.

Nevada and Atlantic City continue to expand the number of casinos, and with lotto fever sweeping the country the expansion of casino gambling is inevitable. An article titled "Heartland's Gaming Explosion" by Frank Kolar in the February 1990 *Win* magazine discussed how Iowa, North and South Dakota, Michigan, Wisconsin and Ohio were looking to casino gambling as a solution to the economic crunch. Already, some of Mr. Kolar's predictions have come true. In addition to the states mentioned, Colorado recently legalized gambling on a limited basis in three Rocky Mountain communities. They report business to be booming and many more casinos are planned. Blackjack, slots and video poker are offered at the three mountain towns of Cripple Creek, Central City, and Blackhawk. As of this writing, Cripple Creek is the only town of the three that offers a poker table. There are currently six casinos in

Central City and eight to twelve are planned. Compared to the casinos of Nevada and Atlantic City, these establishments are strictly mom and pop operations. However, the profits from the slots and blackjack tables have exceeded all expectations and there will be no problem getting new investors to open additional casinos. The fever to legalize casino gambling has spread so fast that several states have legalized it and begun operations since the early chapters of this book were written! As with Colorado, all of the states that are legalizing casino gambling are doing so on a limited basis with low-stakes blackjack as the main attraction.

Because the game of blackjack can be beaten, it is the leading game in Nevada and Atlantic City. Blackjack is the featured game at all of the casinos of the "expansion" states and indications are it will continue to be so. Blackjack has come a long way since the legalization of casino gambling in 1931. It is responsible for over 75 percent of the billions of dollars earned annually in the casinos of Nevada and Atlantic City.

In addition to the expansion of casino gambling to other states, the Indian Nations of this country are trading in their bingo parlors for big-time casino gambling. A recent article in the Seattle Times by Emmett Watson details how the Lummi people in Whatcom County intend to open 24-hour casino gambling in a rehabilitated warehouse. Mr. Watson explains the Lummi complex will be the first of several casinos operated by Native Americans throughout the state of Washington. Naturally, blackjack is slated to be the "headliner." Several other Native American groups are gearing up, or have already, to implement casino gambling.

The United States is on the verge of becoming a gambler's paradise. The introduction of state lotteries has broken the ice. Lotto fever has taken this country by storm and has even reached deep into the Bible Belt. Many states see gambling as the only alternative to raising taxes. Politicians no longer have to say, "Read my lips." They merely have to support the lottery! Texas was always steadfastly opposed to any form of lottery, but when confronted with a likely state income tax or a lottery, it too joined the ranks of us sinners (by a two-to-one majority, I might add).

Gambling is no longer considered the fast track to hell. It is looked upon as salvation in a time of need. As with charity raffles and church sponsored bingo games, gambling is viewed as the only viable source of new revenue the taxpayers will tolerate. Casino gambling is currently and will continue to expand through the nineties and into the next century.

The public's fear of organized crime has always been one of the primary deterrents to the legalization of gambling. Through the assurance of tight state controls, as demonstrated by numerous state lotteries, this fear has dwindled. States currently in the process of legalizing casino gambling are being very careful to keep organized crime out. The small towns and riverboats that currently have casino-type gambling operate on a small and controlled scale. The maximum bets allowed are relatively small (as low as $5) and the amounts people are allowed to lose is limited. Let's hope they don't limit the amount we're allowed to win!

The opening up of casino gambling is great news for those of us looking for a better game. As the competition heats up, the casinos will have to offer more liberal rules in the player's favor in order to compete. The New Jersey Casino Control Commission must loosen its controls on the Atlantic City casinos if it expects them to survive. In conjunction, the casinos in Atlantic City will have to wise up and offer patrons a better shake. The cost of food and lodging in the Atlantic City area will have to be significantly reduced if they expect to offer Nevada any competition in a far more competitive market.

The state of Nevada is in great shape to continue to dominate the gambling market. Of the forty-one towns and cities in Nevada that offer gambling, Las Vegas looked to the future, and has become a family-oriented paradise. A recent article in the Baltimore *Sun* by Ted Chan referred to Las Vegas as "Disneyland with dice." He hit the nail on the head! Las Vegas has turned a gambling mecca into one of the fastest growing cities in the United States. Mr. Chan reports that the population of Greater Las Vegas has grown from 460,000 to about 830,000 in the past ten years. He attributes the population increase to affordable housing, low property taxes and no personal income taxes. After all, a guy could feed a family of four a steak dinner at some of the casinos for less than ten dollars! The city of Las Vegas is an excellent family vacation resort. There are more activities than I need mention designed to keep the children happy and safe while the parents are entertained at the gaming tables. MGM Grand Inc. is in the process of building the MGM Grand Hotel and Theme Park. It is expected to contain over 5,000 rooms, a 171,500-square-foot casino and a 33-acre theme park. The premise of the park is advertised to be walk-through Hollywood-style sets of famous streets throughout the world. The theme park will include numerous rides and attractions comparable to those you would find at a Disney World or a Six Flags. The prices for food and lodging are incredibly low in Las Vegas and the fun and excitement cannot be surpassed. A local newsletter titled Las Vegas *Advisor* works with the casinos to offer unbelievable coupons and special discounts, some of which include free rooms, two-dollar steak dinners, free $25 matchplay chips, show and dinner for less than ten dollars, and the list goes on. Don't let all this talk of Las Vegas being family orientated fool you. It is still the highest-stake gambling city in the United States. One of the biggest bets ever made took place at the Horseshoe Club. A gambler walked in and bet $771,000 on a roll of the dice. Most clubs would have refused such a large bet, but not the Horseshoe! The guy won and left with over $1.5 million. A year later, the same guy came back and was allowed to bet one million dollars. He lost this time and committed suicide a month later. You talk about a poor loser! Las Vegas is also known as the home of the World Series of Poker. Several pots have been known to exceed a million dollars.

Travel packages to Reno, Las Vegas, Atlantic City and the Bahamas can be found in the travel section of your local newspapers. Package deals which include airfare, hotel accommodations and much more can be purchased for less then $200! Some packages can be found that cost you literally nothing if only you possess the "front money." The only catch is, upon arriving at the casino you must purchase the stipulated front money worth of chips. There is often no requirement that you gamble with the chips—but if you don't you will most likely never be invited back. Ensure you are aware of all the benefits and requirements before you choose a package. Robin and I used to fly form Orlando, Florida, to Freeport in the Bahamas on weekends. It cost of $30 for lodging, meals and airfare. At that time, the required front money was $300. I believe the front money requirement for the same trip now is over $500. Our bowling league in Orlando flew to Las Vegas for about $300 per person with no front money required. Those who qualified by spending a minimum time at the gaming tables had most of the $300 returned in cash and matchplay chips. The majority of the "too good to be true" packages to various casinos are true! The idea is to get customers into the casino where they almost always lose more than enough to be profitable for the casino. Don't be stupid; take advantage of these packages and then win!

The opening of another major gambling facility along the East Coast is inevitable. Miami has been talking about doing so for years now. Regardless of which city or state makes the first move, we will all be winners. The monopoly that Atlantic City holds on the East Coast will be gone and East Coast gambling will have to improve. Ironically, one of the reasons no East Coast city or state has stepped forward is because of the mess that was made of Atlantic City in its transition to a gambling town. Hopefully, many lessons were learned and the same travesties won't take place. Atlantic City will eventually loosen up and offer the same liberal blackjack rules to be found in Nevada. Another East Coast facility will just make that day come sooner. Competition for the gambling dollar is going to be fun to watch. It will probably be similar to the gas wars of the 1950s. Many of the largest and most extravagant casinos will have a difficult time making their mortgages. I'm sure that Donald Trump is becoming more and more aware of that. The last time I was in Atlantic City there was talk of a couple of larger casinos being in deep financial trouble. When these casinos realize that catering to the masses is more important that sucking up to a few high rollers is when their trolley will get on the right track. I still can't get over that $7 hamburger!

The East Coast cruise line business has already put a small dent in the Atlantic City East Coast monopoly. Some cruise lines have been offering all-day or all-night cruises to "nowhere." The ships simply go out to sea beyond federal jurisdiction, drop anchor and gamble. I found it easier to get a seat at a $5 table on the cruise ships than I did in Atlantic City! It's actually a reasonable deal. For less than a hundred dollars you can enjoy a cruise, be entertained, eat reasonably well and gamble. What else is there? I have to believe that the games are honest. Robin and I have usually done well at their tables. The blackjack rules are comparable to those in Atlantic City. Complimentary drinks are not included, however, The cruises to "nowhere" are family oriented and many activities are scheduled to keep the children occupied if the parents want to gamble. Staterooms are available at additional cost for those who may want to relax in privacy or have a place for the children to nap.

The rules of blackjack are destined to become more and more liberal as competition heats up. I read in a local paper just yesterday that the Four Queens casino in Las Vegas has begun a month-long promotion to pay 2-to-1 on six cards totaling twenty-one or less. Sounds like the good old days! This is just the tip of the iceberg. More and more casinos will allow us to double-down on any two cards. Early "surrender" may even come back to life. Of course, the number of single- and double-deck games available will increase. If you're still foolish enough to be a card counter, don't get too excited. They will never allow the counter to regain the edge; nor will end play ever by resurrected. Those casinos that really want to pack the house may be tempted to try a promotion that lets players split aces more than once! I admit, this is really pushing it, but competition can be a real motivator.

The game of blackjack should not change significantly. Some casinos may go to as many as twelve decks of cards in a double shoe at some tables. This was tried for a while in Atlantic City but was basically a bust. There is some talk of an automatic shuffle machine that will continuously mix the cards. The advantage of such a machine is that more hands per hour can be played. The hard core card counters will have a fit if these machines are ever employed. I have heard them refer to such tactics as "taking the blackjack out of blackjack." Even I would balk at such a significant change to the game. It would be like putting a pitching machine into a baseball game. I like a full shoe of cards. If the distribution happens to be good, I win that many more hands in a row. If the distribution is bad, I move!

System players will always be around. The counters will continue to fight for the anchor seat and rattle their brains trying to determine the running index. They will never admit that counting is hard work and overrated. In fact, there is no doubt in my mind, *Progression Blackjack* will come under a great deal of criticism and flak from numerous card counting gurus. It will also be attacked by the casinos. In no way does a casino like to see a progression system that works. They can very easily cope with the card counters but have no defense for a progression bettor on a roll. I won't go as far as to say that the casinos and the promoters of the count system are in cahoots for fear you may consider me paranoid. But think about it. As long as the public believes that a count system has a greater than 50% chance of defeating the house, they will continue to frequent the blackjack tables. More books and videos are sold and more money is lost at the tables! This has got to go down as one of the greatest hoaxes of all times. It's almost perfect. The news media, entertainment industry and even the Book of Hoyle have fallen into the trap. Don't get me wrong, card counting will produce favorable results, if, and only if, the system is backed by an extremely large bankroll and if the dealer fails to reshuffle when the large bets are made. The count system does, at times, reveal very small advantages in the player's favor. Card counters who are able to make large bets every time the count is in their favor, may come out ahead. The problem is, the bankroll of the average person who buys and learns the count system cannot possibly support the system. It makes no difference to the author of the "system"—he or she has your money. It's good for the casino, they're about to get your money! If all of this sounds paranoid, then call me paranoid. (If you have read this far—I already have your money! Just kidding!) I prefer to call my argument realistic. I have spilled the beans and am willing to suffer the consequences! I am also willing to continue winning money at the blackjack table using my progression system!

As the years go by, new blackjack experts will surface. They will read *Beat the Dealer*, change a few words here and there, and show up on your television screen at two in the morning. The older experts will be smarter. They will "update" previous material and come on earlier at 1 A.M. As long as there's a buck to be made, there will always be a new system. In the case of blackjack, a "new system" simply means a rehash of an old system. I must give the people who teach "shuffle tracking" credit for an original system. I wonder if they really believe that a person can actually watch a dealer shuffle eight decks of cards and determine a good shoe. Does this mean that if I believe it was a good shuffle I should stay with that shoe regardless of how bad the cards run? Raises some good questions, doesn't it! I did get a kick from the discussion of basing one's play on the shuffle. It reminded me of the time Robin and I went to the dog track with some friends. I had spent about a half hour explaining to a friend of mine a fairly good handicapping system. At the conclusion, I asked him what he looked for in a dog. He replied, "My wife and I always bet the dog whose tail hangs the limpest." It's a good thing we weren't betting at a college track meet! From now on, everytime I watch a dealer shuffle I will be thinking about those poor dogs with the limp tails. I sure hope my friend didn't have to pay money for that system! I was afraid to ask him.

The states that legalize casino gambling on a limited basis such as Colorado, will always maintain tight controls over the games. Blackjack will dominate, followed by slot machines and poker. The table limits will always remain relatively low. The blackjack games will be mostly single- and double-deck. Once again, the counter will be out of luck because of the extremely small betting spread. The progression system will work very well. One simply needs to base the minimum base line bet on 1/10 of the maximum allowed bet. It will probably take the casino until hell freezes over or until the Seattle Mariners win the World Series, whichever comes first, to remove $200 from the progression player's pockets! I expect these new casinos to be a lot of fun. I am very anxious to give them a try. As I stated in the Introduction, blackjack should be simple, exciting, fun and profitable. The action in the "Ma and Pa" casinos will provide all of these things. About the only thing that may be missing is the free drinks!

I am really thrilled at the notion that the Indian Nations are getting into the casino gambling business. If they do for casino gambling what they have done for the bingo industry, Nevada and Atlantic City had better stand by! They turned a small-time game like bingo into a multimillion dollar enterprise. There are Indian bingo parlors that pay out millions of dollars! I am not well versed on the controls associated with an Indian reservation, but I believe they are exempt from state and most federal control. With such huge profits at stake from casino gambling, I seriously doubt that they would jeopardize their reputation by running dishonest games.

The future of blackjack looks great! Always keep in mind that it is a game and not a religion. Play to have fun and don't ever expect to make a living at it. The number of professionals that actually make a living playing blackjack could probably hold a convention in a closet. It's a good bet that there are more blackjack authors than there are professional players. The idea that thousands of people are making a living from blackjack is just one more aspect of the card counting myth. Give the Progression Blackjack system a fair shot. Practice at home as discussed in the Home Improvement chapter. Go to the nearest blackjack table and give them hell! Most of all, have a great time, win lots of money, and never lose more than you can afford!

Thanks for putting up with my ramblings and sometimes warped sense of humor. Please, if you're from Atlantic City, don't take it personally.

GOOD LUCK

P.S. If you're interested in craps, take a break and then read Appendix A.

10

The Feedback Exam

Several years ago I had the pleasure of working with an outstanding naval engineering officer. We worked together in the supervision and training of Navy Propulsion Plant Operators. Our assignment took place aboard a nuclear-powered aircraft carrier during the construction and early operational phase of the ship. The Commander taught me that the training technique employed by nearly every football coach in the country was a model to be emulated. We used this proven "coaching technique" to train and prepare a group of young sailors to safely operate and maintain a complex nuclear-powered propulsion plant. Our efforts proved to be highly effective, as demonstrated by the record-setting performance of our propulsion plant personnel during various postconstruction operational tests and inspections.

The coaching technique that I advocate consists of four distinct phases, as follows:

1. INSTRUCTION: The initial training phase consisting of books, training aids, classroom instruction, demonstrations, etc.
2. FEEDBACK: Having the trainee demonstrate the level of knowledge obtained through written/verbal exams, drills, walkthroughs, etc.

3. PRACTICE: Having the trainee hone his or her skills through repetition and practice.
4. THE FINAL EXAM: Using the knowledge acquired for the purpose intended, whether it be passing a college final exam, operating a nuclear propulsion plant, or a satisfactory performance on the job.

By now you're probably wondering what the heck is going on! What do football and power plants have to do with blackjack? What's Dahl up to? I thought this was a blackjack book!

Hold one! Let me explain.

The goal of Progression Blackjack is to provide you with the instruction, practice and feedback necessary to play winning blackjack. Your final exam entails the proper application of the strategies taught in this book. Thus far you have completed the instruction and may or may not have completed your "homework." As yet, no feedback has been required of you. The feedback and practice phases are essential if one expects to excel in any instructional program. Chronological order is not critical in the case of blackjack, as it might be in football or in the training of a nuclear power plant operator. If you have conducted practice sessions as outlined in the Home Improvement chapter, the feedback phase should be a "piece of cake."

The Feedback Exam will provide you with self-feedback to gauge your current understanding of the information presented in this book. As with all how-to books, only you can determined when you're ready to take on the final exam. This exercise should be viewed as a tool to enhance your knowledge and expose any weak areas. For your convenience, I indicate and discuss the correct answer immediately following each question. (Having to flip pages to find the answer key is a bummer!) To help keep you honest, I intentionally avoided printing the corresponding letter for the correct answer. The exam includes questions covering all major topics and strategies discussed in Progression Blackjack.

Each question provides you with a short scenario containing enough information to correctly answer the question. When double-down, split or early surrender are offered as possible answers, they should be considered as options authorized under "house rules." In general, most casinos limit double-down situations and do not offer early surrender. To prepare you for all situations you may encounter, liberal rules are incorporated in this exam. If I were a betting man, I'd wager that you will find the following exam both beneficial and fun. Have at it!

Casino Blackjack

1. The game of blackjack can at times give a player better odds of winning than craps because_____.

A. Larger wagers may be made at the blackjack table.
B. Blackjack dealers will often assist the player.
C. The house percentage is always fixed in craps but may vary in favor of the player in blackjack.
D. The game of blackjack is easier to understand.

Answer: Most people do agree that blackjack is easier to learn and understand than craps. However, that has nothing to do with the odds of winning. In craps, the odds never vary and are in favor of the house. In blackjack, odds can shift in favor of the player as cards are depleted.

2. The best prices on food and lodging are most likely to be found in

_____.

A. Nevada.
B. Atlantic City.
C. Freeport in the Bahamas.
D. Aboard a cruise ship.

Answer: Cruise ships are excellent vacation values. However, the prices of food and lodging at various casinos in Nevada cannot be beat.

3. Select the statement that most accurately describes the card cutting procedure.

A. The cut made by the player determines the first card to be dealt, the cut made by the dealer determines when play from the shoe is concluded.
B. The cut made by the player determines when play from the shoe is concluded, the cut by the dealer determines the first card to be dealt.

C. Multiple-deck shoes are not cut.
D. The player determines the first card to be dealt and when play from the shoe is concluded.

Answer: The casino is not about to let a player determine how many cards are to be dealt to the players! They do allow the player to make the cut that determines the first card played. The dealer's cut determines how many cards will be played prior to the next shuffle.

4. The proper procedure to indicate that you desire a hit is to _____.

A. Brush your finger(s) on top of the nearest card or say, "Hit me."
B. Wave your hand over the top of the cards or say, "Hit me."
C. No hand or finder signals are accepted. You must say, "Hit me."
D. Brush your finger(s) on the table below your cards or say "Hit me."

Answer: Very few casinos allow a player to touch their cards. A wave of the hand over the cards is considered a request to stay. A gently brush on the table below your cards is the ticket!

5. You receive a total of 15, the dealer has a 6 up and you stay. The dealer turns up a 10 as his hole card. What action must be taken by the dealer?

A. The dealer must stay and you are beat by the 16.
B. The dealer may hit or stay at his discretion.
C. The dealer must hit to a total of 17 or greater.
D. The answer is dependent on "house rules" which cannot be determined by the information given.

Answer: One of the most basic rules in blackjack is that the house must hit to 17 or greater. Some casinos once used to allow the dealer to stay on a soft 17 but nearly all today require a hard 17. Keep in mind, this is to the casino's advantage. That is why you should always hit to a hard 17 or greater if the dealer has a standing card showing!

6. The dealer and you both reach a total hand value of 20. What happens?

A. You have "pushed" and no money is exchanged.
B. All ties go to the dealer and you lose the wager.
C. All ties go to the player and you win the wager.
D. The dealer wins 1/2 of your original wager on a push.

Answer: If the house wins on pushes you had better go somewhere else! If you find a house that pays players on a push, give me a call! This isn't a runner going to first base, no one wins on a tie. No money is exchanged.

7. The proper procedure to indicate that you desire to split a pair of 8's is to _____. (Cards are dealt face-up from a shoe.)

A. Place an additional wager equal to the original wager on top of the original wager; inform the dealer to split.
B. Place an additional wager equal to the original wager beside the original wager; inform the dealer to split.
C. Separate the 8s and place the additional wager beside the original wager; inform the dealer to split.
D. Remove the original wager and place up to twice the value of the original wager on the table; inform the dealer to split.

Answer: Never touch the original wager or the cards unless you want your hand slapped! Place the additional bet alongside the original and the dealer will move the cards.

8. Select the statement which is true concerning the splitting of pairs.

A. The player receives cards on one of the split cards one at a time until it is "good" or "busts." The second split card is played out after the first.
B. The player receives cards on each of the split cards alternately.
C. Aces may be split more than once.
D. Fives should always be split.

Answer: The vast majority of casinos do not allow aces to be split more than once. You should never ever split 5's! You always play out the first card split before receiving a card on the second card split.

9. The dealer has an 8 up. You receive a pair of 8's. You split and receive a 3 on the first 8. What action should be taken?

A. Take another hit.
B. Stand.
C. You would not have split 8's against an 8.
D. Double-down on the 11.

Answer: Eights should be split against a 2-8. You are allowed to double-down if the first card on a split card gives you a total of 10 or 11 (some casinos allow a double-down on any two cards). Always double-down when you have a two-card total of 11. You must go for it and double-down! If the casino does not allow you to double-down after a split, go to another casino.

10. You have bet $10 and receive a two-card total of 11. Select the procedure to be used.

A. Place an additional $20 behind the original $10 and inform the dealer of your desire to double-down.
B. Place an additional $20 on top of the original $10 and inform the dealer of your desire to double-down.
C. Place an additional $10 on top of the original $10 and inform the dealer of your desire to double-down.
D. Place an additional $10 behind the original $10 and inform the dealer of your desire to double-down.

Answer: Once again, you are not allowed to touch the original bet. On a split or double-down players are only allowed to make an additional wager up to the amount of the original wager. Thus, you would place $10 behind the original wager.

11.You wager $10, receive a pair of aces and split. On the first ace your receive a jack of spades. On the second ace you receive a 9. Dealer hits to a 19. How much money do you win?

A. $25 (3/2 on the blackjack)
B. $10
C. $20
D. $40

Answer: 3/2 is only paid on your initial two-card total of 21. In this case you win a total of $20.

12. Dealer has a 5 showing. You receive a two-card total of 9 and are allowed to double-down. You now receive a 2 for a total of 11. What action do you take?

A. Double-down again.
B. No other action can be taken.
C. Take a hit.
D. None of the above.

Answer: Players are only allowed to double-down on a two-card total. You could not double-down again. Players are only allowed one card on a double-down. You could not take a hit. All you can do is hope the dealer busts. In other words, no other action can be taken.

13. The practice of dealers peeking at their hole card was terminated because _____.

A. Questions were raised concerning cheating.
B. A 4 often required a second look.
C. Small bends were sometimes put in the cards.
D. All of the above.

Answer: Experts were able to gain information because of small bends put in the cards and by second peeks often required when a 4 was in the hole. Some dealers would look at the hole card when there was no need to. This raised questions concerning cheating by the dealer. "All of the above" sounds like a winner!

14. Dealer has a King showing. You have wagered $10, receive a two-card total of 11, and double-down. You receive a Jack of

Hearts on the double. The dealer has an ace in the hole. What happens?

A. You lose $20.
B. You push.
C. You lose $10.
D. You should have taken insurance.

Answer: The dealer received a two-card total of 21 which is a natural blackjack. You must lose because you did not have a blackjack. The good news is that you only lose the original wager of $10 and get to keep the double-down wager. Insurance is only offered when the dealer has an ace showing.

15. Dealer has an ace showing. The player next to you bet $100 and has a two-card total of 20. The player takes maximum insurance. The dealer has a 4 in the hole and draws a 6. How did this player fare?

A. Lost $150.
B. Lost $50.
C. Won $50.
D. Broke even.

Answer: If you had taken the insurance I'd have tanned your fanny! The player bucked the odds by taking insurance. Lost the insurance bet and the original bet for a grand total of $150. Remember, up to half of the original bet can be wagered on insurance. I'm surprised that casinos don't let players bet more on insurance. I should probably tan my own fanny for giving them the idea! After all, there are people who will bet the farm on this sucker bet!

16. Dealer has an ace showing, you have wagered $200 and have a blackjack. You take insurance and the dealer has the 10-value card in the hole. How do you make out?

A. Push.
B. You win $200.

C. You win $300.
D. None of the above.

Answer: Having a blackjack is the only time I advocate taking insurance. Though you are bucking the odds, you are betting on a sure thing! You push on the blackjack but win 2/1 on the insurance bet. If my math is correct, this equates to a $200 profit on the hand. Not a bad return on a sure thing! If the healer did not have the 10, you would still have gained $200—a $100 loss on the insurance bet and a gain of 3/2 on the original bet.

17. The player who never hits on 12 or greater, regardless of the dealer's up card is _____.

A. Destined to lose.
B. Playing against the odds.
C. Uneducated in the game of blackjack.
D. All of the above.

Answer: The only thing I wish I had added is stupid! These players may have lucky streaks that will only temporarily delay the loss of their total bankroll. As you may have guessed, the answer is "all of the above."

18. The most confusing aspect of blackjack to the novice player is the _____.

A. Split strategy.
B. Soft hands.
C. Double-down strategy.
D. Insurance.

Answer: The novice player is not confused about splits and double-downs. They just don't take advantage of them. They rarely get confused about insurance because they always take it! They have a very difficult time with soft hands, however. Give them two aces and a 5 and watch them squirm!

19. The average blackjack player loses the majority of the time because _____.

A. They have no idea of what they are doing.
B. They rarely tip the dealers.
C. They bet the same amount each hand.
D. All of the above.

Answer: Most players have a basic understanding of the game. The problem is, they always bet the same amount on each hand and don't understand that the dealers are bound to win more hands in the long run.

20. To beat the casino at blackjack, one must _____.

A. Take advantage of all split situations.
B. Take advantage of all double-down situations.
C. Win more money while winning than is lost while losing.
D. All of the above.

Answer: If there is any major theme stressed throughout this book, it would have to be "all of the above."

A Winning Play Strategy

1. The good blackjack players make their own luck through _____.

A. Intuition.
B. Larger bankrolls.
C. Proper play.
D. All of the above.

Answer: I have tried to wean you from the use of intuition. If often runs contrary to proper play strategy. A larger bankroll has no bearing on the result of a given hand, but an adequate bankroll is essential to be able to play. Proper play will steer the luck your way!

2. Select the incorrect statement concerning basic play strategy.

A. If the dealer's up card is a "standing card," hit until your total is 17 or greater.
B. When the dealer has a "standing card" up, assume a 10-value card in the hole.
C. House rules require the dealer to hit to 17 or more.
D. When the dealer's up card is a "stiff," do not hit if your total is 12 or more.

Answer: Basic strategy assumes a 10-value card in the hole even though the odds are against it. When the dealer has a standing card showing, you must hit to 17 or greater. To be more specific, you must hit to a "hard" 17 or more. If the dealer's up card is a stiff, you should never risk a bust except when you have a total of 12, against a 2 or 3 up. All casinos require the dealer to hit to 17 or greater. Most casinos require the dealer to hit to a "hard" 17 or more. When the dealer's up card is a "stiff," do not hit if your total is 13 or more (not 12) is a correct statement.

3. Why does the house require the dealer to hit to a 17 or more?

A. It is to their advantage.
B. To give the player better odds.
C. To attract more players.
D. All of the above.

Answer: Casinos are in the business to make money. It is a significant advantage for the dealer to hit to 17 or greater. In the early years of blackjack, dealers were required to stay on any 17 or greater. To improve the advantage, most casinos have adopted the requirement to hit to a hard 17 or more.

4. The primary advantage a blackjack table has over the players is _____.

A. The players must hit first.
B. The house is required to hit to 17 or greater.

C. Dealers are better trained than the average player.
D. The house has no advantage.

Answer: Proper play requires the player to hit to a 17 or greater (assuming the dealer has a standing card up) to counter the house rule requiring the dealer to hit to 17. The dealers' knowledge of the game has no bearing on the outcome of a hand because they are bound to abide by the house hitting and standing rules, regardless of the player's hand. The casino prospers at blackjack primarily because players are required to risk busting first. I have seen many occasions where all players have busted and lost their wagers without the dealer ever having to turn over the hole card!

5. The dealer's up card is a 7. You receive a soft 17. What play do you make?

A. Stand.
B. Hit.
C. Double-down.
D. B or C.

Answer: Always hit to a soft 17 regardless of the dealer's up card! If the dealer has a 3-6 up, you should double-down. The house usually requires the dealer to hit to a hard 17 or greater; so should you. There is greater than a 62% chance of improving a soft 17.

6. The dealer's up card is a 10. You receive a soft 19. What play do you make?

A. Stand
B. Hit
C. Double down.
D. B or C.

Answer: A 19 is a good hand! Always stand on a soft 19 or 20. The average dealer hand is slightly over 18. Only if the dealer's hole card is a 10 or ace will you crash and burn. Luckily for us, the odds are against it.

7. The dealer's up card is a 9. You receive a soft 18. What play do you make

A. Stand.
B. Hit.
C. Double-down.
D. B or C.

Answer: The odds go with hitting a soft 18 against a 9 or 10. If the dealer shows a 3-6, you should double-down. A 2, 7, 8, or ace up calls for you to stand.

8. Many casinos no longer allow players to double-down on any two cards because _____.

A. It slowed down the game.
B. It confused the players.
C. It was to the player's advantage.
D. It was to the player's disadvantage.

Answer: The ability to double-down on any two cards can be a valuable tool in the hands of a knowledgeable player. The casinos became wise to the advantage gained by the players and terminated this ability. As competition has heated up among the casinos, the liberal double-down rules are making a return. The ability to double-down on any two cards should be a primary concern in your casino selection. One reason casinos are willing to reintroduce the liberal double-down rules is because they know that the average player is not knowledgeable enough to take full advantage of them. Know the double-down charts!

9. The dealer has an ace up. You receive a two-card total of 10. What action do you take?

A. Take insurance and hit.
B. Take insurance and double-down.
C. Hit.
D. Double-down.

Answer: Never take insurance unless you have a blackjack! Double-down on a 10 against an ace but do not double-down against a 10-value card. If the dealer has the natural you will get the double-down wager back. Most players never double against the ace; most players lose!

10. The dealer has a 10 up. You receive a two-card total of 11. What action do you take?

A. Double-down
B. Hit.
C. Surrender.
D. A or B, depending on the size of the wager.

Answer: Always double-down on an 11 regardless of the size of the wager. You will lose some of these bets but will come out ahead in the long run.

11. Soft double-down strategy relies on _____.

A. The player's hand being improved.
B. The size of the bankroll.
C. The dealer busting.
D. A and C.

Answer: The size of your bankroll should never have an influence on play strategy. It only determines the betting progression you can afford to employ. Soft double-downs are only recommended against stiffs. Therefore, soft double-down strategy is based on both the chance of improving one's hand and the odds of the dealer busting.

12. The dealer has a 4 up. You receive a soft 13. What action do you take?

A. Hit.
B. Stand.
C. Double-down.
D. A or C.

Answer: Your chance of improving the soft 13 is about 39%. The odds of the dealer busting is good with a 4 up. This combination is too good to pass up. Double-down! Since the odds of improving your hand is only 39%. only double-down against a 4, 5 or 6 to ensure the dealer's odds of busting are good.

13. The dealer has a 7 up. You receive a soft 17. What action do you take?

A. Hit.
B. Stand.
C. Double-down.
D. A or C.

Answer: Soft 17 should only be doubled-down against a 3, 4, 5, or 6. The odds are in your favor to hit until you have a hard 17 or greater, against the 7.

14. The dealer has a 2 up. You receive a two-card total of 9. What action do you take?

A. Hit.
B. Stand.
C. Double-down.
D. A or C.

Answer: The 9 should be doubled-down against 2-6. The two-card total of 8 should only be doubled against a 5 or 6. If a double-down is not recommended, then hit to a hard 17 or greater.

15. The winning strategy of splitting pairs is used to _____.

A. Win both hands.
B. Split to avoid a bust and possibly win both hands.
C. Break even by winning one hand and losing the other.
D. All of the above.

Answer: A pair should never be split if likely to lose both hands.

Nor should a pair be split if it requires breaking up a winning hand. All of the answers listed are legitimate reasons to split pairs.

16. One exception to always splitting aces is _____.

A. There are no exceptions, always split aces.
B. Against the dealer's ace.
C. Against 10-value cards.
D. B and C.

Answer: Not much to discuss. Always split aces!

17. Select the statement that most accurately describes when 10's should be split.

A. When the deck is rich in high-value cards.
B. Never.
C. Against 2-9.
D. Single-deck play only.

Answer: Twenty is a winning hand and must never be split up. You will never encounter a situation that benefits by splitting 10;s.

18. The dealer has a 10 up. You receive a pair of 9's. What action do you take?

A. Split.
B. Split and double-down on each.
C. Stand.
D. Hit.

Answer: Splitting 9's against a 10 or ace is a losing proposition. It could easily result in losing two hands. Stand and hope for the best!

19. The dealer has a 5 up. You receive a pair of 9's. What action do you take?

A. Split.
B. Split and double-down on each.

C. Stand.
D. Hit.

Answer: Split and double-down sounds like the winner! The problem is, casinos only allow double-downs on two-card totals. In this case, you will only be allowed to split. You can always hope to receive a 2 on one or both of the splits and then double-down.

20. Many experts advocate always splitting 8's. *Progression Black-jack* does not because ———.

A. 16 is not that hard a total to hit to.
B. You should not risk losing double against dealer's 9-A.
C. 8's are unlucky.
D. All of the above.

Answer: 16 is a terrible hand to hit to! I cringe every time I am forced into it. On the other hand, I am not about to double my losses when facing a 9-A. It sure is nice when the old 5-spot is the card I receive!

21. The dealer has a 7 up. You receive a pair of 7's. What action do you take.

A. Split.
B. Stand.
C. Hit.
D. Surrender.

Answer: 14 is not a good hand to hit to. Against the 7 I hope to at least break even by splitting. Surrender should only be used when you are having to hit a lousy stiff (15 or 16) against a dealer's strong standing card (10 or A). It should never be used when splitting is a viable solution. Split 7's against the 2-7 and hit otherwise.

22. The dealer has a 2 up. You receive a pair of 6's. What action do you take?

A. Split.

B. Stand.
C. Hit.
D. Surrender.

Answer: Basic strategy taught you to hit a 12 against a 2 or 3. In this case, however, your best bet is to split the 6's.

23. The dealer has an 8 up. You receive a pair of 5's. What action do you take?

A. Split.
B. Stand.
C. Hit.
D. Double-down.

Answer: Never split 5's. You have a double-down situation. Go for it!

24. The casino pays us 2/1 on a successful insurance bet. The actual odds of a 10-value card in the hole is approximately _____.

A. 1.5/1.
B. 2/1.
C. 2.5/1.
D. 3/1.

Answer: The casino is willing to pay us 2/1 on a 2.5/1 proposition. That's might neighborly of them.

25. Select the statement that is true concerning proper play strategy.

A. Always take insurance.
B. Always split aces.
C. Never split 10's.
D. B and C.

Answer: If in doubt at this point in time, please reread the book!

Systems

1. Most blackjack systems fail to ensure that _____.

A. Aces are split.
B. 8's are split.
C. Larger bets are made while winning.
D. Larger bets are made when the "chance" of winning is in the player's advantage.

Answer: Most systems teach the correct play strategy. The biggest flaw with the majority of the systems is that they do not ensure that the larger bets are made when on a winning streak. They merely advocate betting more when the "odds" indicate a greater chance of winning. The major problem with this is that the odds rarely warrant larger bets. When they do, the advantage is extremely slim and not worth the risk (unless you are working with a huge bankroll). In a multiple-deck game, the average player rarely gains an advantage warranting an increased bet. This results in usually making the same wager, a sure road to defeat!

2. Assuming an unlimited bankroll and no table limit, which blackjack system would you select?

A. Positive Progression.
B. Point Count.
C. Ten Count.
D. Negative Progression.

Answer: There is no comparison! The negative progression, more commonly referred to as the Martingale system, would "eat the casino's lunch" under these condition. If allowed to double-up after each loss, you could not possibly lose! Sooner or later you would win a hand. One may be able to come up with the unlimited bankroll, but we will never see a casino offer an unlimited table limit. The negative progression system is ideal under unrealistic conditions but does not hold up in the real world!

3. Starting with a $25 bet, how many hands in a row can you lose before reaching a $500 table limit employing the Martingale system?

A. 4.
B. 5.
C. 6.
D. 7.

Answer: The sixth bet would have to be $800. Therefore, the answer is 5. After five losses you would be down $775 and the most you could bet on the next hand would be $500. It sure doesn't sound like a winning system to me!

4. If a deck of cards is short in 5's, the advantage goes to _____.

A. The Player.
B. The House.
C. There is no advantage.
D. Depends on how many decks of cards.

Answer: There is a very slight mathematical advantage to the player when a deck is short in 5's. This was the basis of the early 5-count system. The advantage panned out to be so small that this system eventually faded away.

5. Most card counting systems revolve around the theory that _____.

A. An educated player can beat the dealer every time.
B. The player should never risk busting.
C. The richer a deck is in high-value cards, the greater the player's advantage.
D. All of the above.

Answer: All currently accepted counting systems are based on the fact that a 10-rich deck is in favor of the player. This is a valid contention that made many a player rich during the card counter "golden years." As the casinos grew wise to the advantage, they were able to take appropriate countermeasures to reduce the advantage. The various card counting systems teach similar techniques to detect when the deck(s) are rich in tens. Through multiple decks and quick shuffles, the casinos minimize the occurrences of 10-rich situations. As a counter, I have gone through numerous shoes and rarely encountered 10-rich situations warranting any significant increase in bet. A blackjack system that essentially has a player make the same bet on every hand is doomed to failure!

6. At one time, the card counters greatest weapon was _____.

A. End play.
B. Strategy charts.
C. The ability to split aces more than once.
D. Large bankrolls.

Answer: The ability to re-split aces was definitely an advantage. However, the large sums of money old-timers were able to win came from endplay. In a one-on-one situation with the dealer, a player would often encounter situations where he or she knew that they could not lose. Having a pair of 10's with the dealer's 9 up, knowing that only 10-value cards are left in the deck was quite an advantage. A situation like this was good justification to split 10's! The end play stories go on and on. End play was taking a bite out of the casino. I assure you, it didn't take the casinos long to figure out that they had a problem!

7. To determine the "index number" using the point count system entails _____.

A. Assigning values to each card.
B. Maintaining a running count.
C. Dividing the count by the number of remaining cards.
D. All of the above.

Answer: You talk about taking the fun out of the game! To think that I wasted thousands of hours doing all of the above!

8. In the point count system, the "index number" is used to _____.

A. Determine the wager to be made.
B. Determine when deviation from basic strategy is required.
C. A and B.
D. Determine if the dealer is cheating.

Answer: The index number is used primarily to determine what your next bet should be. It can also indicate when a deviation from the basic strategy is required. At least that's what the blackjack card counting gurus teach. In reality, the index number rarely advocates a significant change in bet and almost never indicates that a change in strategy is required. To do so much work for such little return, what a waste!

9. The use of multiple-deck shoes greatly reduced the card counters advantage by _____.

A. Eliminating end play.
B. Reducing the significance of a given index number.
C. Reducing the occurrences of favorable player situations.
D. All of the above.

Answer: If you answered "all of the above," you have earned your degree in "Systems."

10. A more realistic alternative to shuffle tracking is to _____.

A. Bribe the dealer.
B. Use the count system.
C. Move if the cards are running cold.
D. Use the Martingale system.

Answer: Shuffle tracking is a complete waste of time. It looks good on paper but is almost impossible in practice. If the cards aren't shuffled correctly, who cares? If they are going my way, I keep playing. If they are cold, I move. Why would anyone study shuffle tracking? Makes as much sense as a government study on the brain wave patterns of a housefly!

A Winning Progression

1. The key to profitable blackjack is _____.

A. Card counting.
B. Luck.
C. Risking the minimal bet while losing, and increasing the bet while winning.
D. Employing the negative progression system when losing, and the positive progression system while winning.

Answer: Luck is an important factor. However, betting more while winning than is lost while losing is the answer. Card counting and the negative progression have only made a few authors rich in recent years, not players.

2. The most significant aspect of any blackjack system is _____.

A. The betting strategy.
B. The double-down strategy.
C. The split strategy.
D. The hard hitting strategy.

Answer: The meat and potatoes of all blackjack systems is the betting strategy. Without a winning bet strategy the system is useless. All experts, casinos, computers and knowledgeable players agree with the same basic play strategy. The crucial factor, which few agree on, is the betting strategy. I have little argument with any play strategy published. I do challenge the majority of the betting strategies. To think that so few of these experts fail to recognize that you must bet more while winning then is lost while losing, is beyond me.

3. The primary defense the casino has to deter the positive progression player _____.

A. Multiple-deck shoes.
B. No defense.
C. Quick shuffles.
D. Rule changes.

Answer: Multiple-deck shoes and quick shuffles are no defense against the positive progression system. In fact, the positive progression system was developed because of multiple-deck shoes and quick shuffles! I can't imagine any rule changes that casinos could employ to deter the positive progression player. They would have to be so drastic that they would chase everyone away from the tables. There is absolutely no defense against the positive progression player. If the cards run the right way, the casino is in for a beating. They know it, fear it, but are not about to admit it!

4. After winning _____ hands in a row, the positive progression system guarantees a profit on a given streak.

A. 2.
B. 3.
C. 4.
D. 5.

Answer: The progression taught in *Progression Blackjack* ensures a net gain after winning only two hands in a row. As the number of hands in a row increase, so does the gain. If you were to lose every other hand you would merely break even.

5. The Dahl Progression allows you to _____.

A. Increase your bets while losing.
B. Make large profits when the cards are "hot" and minimize losses when cold.
C. Rely on intuition to determine the bet.
D. Win money regardless of how the luck is going.

Answer: As much as I would like to guarantee that you will always win money, I can't. All I can do is teach you a betting progression that will reap large profits during "hot" streaks and minimize losses when things are going bad. Blackjack is a gamble. If your luck is terrible, you will lose.

6. You bet the first $50 of the $10 progression. Split aces and win on both. What is your next bet?

A. The second $50.
B. The first $70.
C. $10.
D. The second $70.

Answer: You have won $100. The jump bet rules require that you skip two levels of the progression (unless the money you would be risking is more than you just received). You therefore skip the second $50 and the first $70 and bet the second $70.

7. You bet the first $50 of the $10 progression and win with a blackjack. What is your next bet?

A. The second $50.
B. The first $70.
C. $10.
D. The second $70.

Answer: You received $75 on the blackjack. The jump bet rules reouire that you skip one level of the progression. Your next bet should be the first $70.

8. You bet the second $30 of the $10 progression. You receive a tow-card total of 11, double-down and win. What is your next bet?

A. $10.
B. The first $50.
C. The second $50.
D. The first $70.

Answer: You received $60. The jump bet rules require that you skip two levels of the progression unless the money you would be risking is more than you just received. Skipping two levels puts you at the first $70 bet which is more than the $60 won. You should therefore bet the second $50.

9. You bet the first $10 of the $5 progression. Split 8's, lose on the first 8, receive a 3 on the second, and complete a successful double-down. What is your next bet?

A. The first $5.
B. The second $10.
C. The first $15.
D. The second $15.

Answer: The net gain on the hand was $10. You should therefore move to the next level of the progression which is the second $10. If you have broken even on the hand, the next bet would be a repeat of the first $10. If you lost money on the hand, you would be required to go back to the first $5.

10. The table is hot! You are several thousand ahead using the $25 progression. You lose at the first $175 level. What should you do?

A. Quit while ahead.
B. Repeat the first $175 bet.
C. Bet $25.
D. Bet the second $175 bet.

Answer: Never quit while you are on a hot streak! You lost the hand, so go back to the start of the progression. It may take some willpower to bet a measly $25 when you're thousands ahead, but after all, that's how you *got* ahead!

11. The table is hot! The dealer is busting left and right! You have just won your second $20 bet on the $10 progression. A new dealer arrived to "cool" the table. What should you do?
A. Bet the first $30 bet.
B. Bet $10.
C. Sit out a few hands to check out the dealer.
D. Move to another table.

Answer: There is no doubt about it! The progression couldn't care less who's dealing. Make the next bet in the progression and stay on that roll! If the table cools off, consider a move. Never quit or reduce the bet in the middle of a winning progression.

12. The purpose of the jump bet rules is to _____.

A. Help recoup your losses.
B. Compensate for multiple-deck shoes.
C. Allow rapid advancement up the betting ladder.
D. All of the above.

Answer: The only reason I introduced the jump/skip bet rules was to increase your profits during a hot streak. I do this by allowing a more rapid advancement by the betting ladder when things are going good.

13. You are using the $10 progression. Assuming no splits, double-downs, or blackjacks, what is your profit after losing the 1st $70 bet?
A. $180.
B. $160.
C. $280.
D. $80.

Answer: Sorry about the question! I wanted to make you spend a little time with the progression. If my math is correct, you should have come up with $180. In the real world, you would most likely win much more with splits, double-downs and blackjacks.

14. While playing the $25 progression I would be as cool as a cucumber after losing a $250 bet because _____.

A. I have a secure full-time job.
B. I like to lose.
C. My parents are rich.
D. I have won a great deal of money by reaching a $250 bet.

Answer: Depending on the number of splits, double-downs, and blackjacks, a player will have close to $1,000 profit from such a run. You will soon discover that the larger the bet you lose, the sweeter the pie! Nothing beats being a high roller on house money!

15. The Progression Blackjack System is superior to the Card Counting System because _____.

A. It assures that more money is bet while winning than is lost while losing.
B. It is not weakened by multiple-deck shoes.
C. It is not affected by quick shuffles.
D. The casinos have no defense against it.
E. It requires a smaller bankroll.
F. It allows you to be a high roller on a small budget.
G. It is more fun.
H. It does not require memorization, addition, and division.
I. It is easier to learn.
J. It makes more sense.
K. It works.
L. All of the above and more.

Answer: This is a freebie. "All of the above and more!"

Money Management

1. *Progression Blackjack* advocates which following "win goal"?

A. 20% of the session money.
B. 20% of the total bankroll.
C. No limit.
D. $1,000.

Answer: Setting a win goal of 20% on the typical session money or bankroll is unrealistic and ridiculous! The idea is good for filling the pages of a book or video, that's about it. When I hit the tables, I take what I can afford to lose. I quit when it's time to leave! Doesn't most everyone? I know that my progression can, under the right circums-tances, make far more than a 20% profit. Perhaps the advocates of win goals are not true believers in their systems! Are we gullible enough to believe that they actually practice what they preach? Would they quit after winning 20% of their session money? If I wanted an additional 20% income I would get a second job. Blackjack is a game; we play for fun and try to win as much as we can. To set a small win goal is contrary to why we play. Go for the gusto, win as much as you can!

2. The typical money management system requires the minimum bet be _____ of the player's bankroll.

A. 1/50–1/100th.
B. 1/100–1/200th.
C. 1/150–1/500th.
D. 1/150–1/1,000th.

Answer: The majority of the systems I have studied require the player to have a bankroll of $750 to $5,000 in order to play at a $5 table! This equates to 1/150–1/1,000th. of the bankroll. I guess we should all go out and take a second mortgage on our houses in order to play! *Progression Blackjack* recommended a minimum bet of only 1/50th of the bankroll. You can affort to play a $5 table with as little as a $250 bankroll.

3. Your total gambling bankroll is $1,200 to be spread over a three-day period. You intend to play two sessions per day. How much money should you risk at the first session?

A. $200.
B. $400.
C. $800.
D. $1,200.

Answer: You must use common sense and good discipline. You obviously want the bankroll to last three days. With two sessions per day, divide the total bankroll by six.

4. After the first session (described in question number 3) you are $300 ahead. What would be your session allowance now?

A. $200.
B. $300.
C. $400.
D. $500.

Answer: The bankroll has grown to $1,500 with five sessions remaining. Keep up the good work but risk no more than $300 at the next session.

5. Regarding previous question numbers 3 and 4, what is the maximum betting progression allowed by *Progression Blackjack* at sessions 1 and 2.

A. $2 and $2.
B. $2 and $5.
C. $5 and $5.
D. $10 and $25.

Answer: If you had a bankroll of $1,200 to be risked at only one session, you qualify for the $10 progression. After gaining $300 you became eligible to use the $25 progression. As determined in question 3, however, the bankroll supporting the first session is $200, which only qualifies for a $2 progression. The bankroll for the second session became $300, which allows a $5 progression. It's important to note that the money you are willing to lose at a given session should be used to determine the progression to use, not the total bankroll you brought to town. If you attempt to play a $10 table with only $200 to lose, it could be a very short session!

6. You arrive in Atlantic City on an overnight junket. Cards have been good and you are $75 ahead using the $5 progression. Your total bankroll is now $375. You like the table and the people you are playing with. The pit boss informs the table that the table minimum will be raised to $10 at the start of the next shoe. What should you do?

A. Quit for the evening. You have exceeded a 20% win goal.
B. Stay at the table. Try the $10 progression.
C. Plead with the pit boss not to raise the table minimum.
D. Move to a $5 table.

Answer: I assure you that this is a very realistic scenario. One New Year's Eve I was foolish enough to play a progression my wallet could not support. You must always play within your means. Get up and find a $5 table! The casino would like nothing better than for you to remain with inadequate funds to support your bets.

7. In *Progression Blackjack*, the minimum bet is based on (a) _____ and the maximum bet is based on (b)_____.

A. (a) the bankroll (b) the number of hands won in a row.
B. (a) the bankroll (b) intuition.
C. (a) gut feeling (b) luck.
D. (a) the bankroll (b) current profit.

Answer: The progression you are allowed to play determines the minimum bet, which is solely dependant on the size of the bankroll. The number of hands won in a row during a given run determines the maximum bet you can make.

8. Two hours into the $5 progression and you are $85 ahead. Select the action to take after losing several hands in a row.

A. Quit while still ahead.
B. Move to another table or casino.
C. Try the $10 progression, your luck is bound to change.
D. Stay at the table until broke.

Answer: Cards tend to run in streaks. Some tables run hot and cold. Some shoes favor the house and others favor the players. After losing several hands in a row, I would certainly move to greener pastures!

9. You and your spouse plan to play the $10 tables. What is the minimum bankroll required to support the two of you?

A. $250.
B. $500.
C. $1,000.
D. $2,000

Answer: It is easy for a couple to overlook the fact that they both plan on playing. They look at the recommended bankroll table and expect to play the $10 progression with $500. Keep in mind, that's $500 each! $1,000 will do just fine.

10. Select the statement that best explains why it is important to adhere to the minimum bankroll requirements.

A. Only rich people should be allowed to play blackjack.
B. A minimum bankroll is required to survive when the cards are not going your way.
C. A minimum bankroll is required to allow a more rapid betting progression.
D. All of the above.

Answer: As much as we hate to admit it, there will be times when the cards keep going the wrong way. The minimum bankroll requirements are to help you weather the storm during such periods. I have seen people make $100 wagers with a $500 bankroll! It sure doesn't take them long to go home broke. The recommended bankrolls should give you a fighting chance to hang around long enough for the tide to turn.

Odds and Ends

1. The key to gaining proficiency with the concepts taught in *Progression Blackjack* is _____.

A. Obtaining 100% on the feedback exam.
B. Practice.
C. Memorization of the bankroll chart.
D. Rereading the book.

Answer: As with most other skills, there is no substitute for practice. The feedback exam was written to assist you by stressing major points. It is not designed as a substitute for practice. I would do quite well on a written exam covering the proper golf swing. Performance on the golf course is another story!

2. During the practice sessions, you should establish _____.

A. The most realistic conditions possible.

B. Who should deal.
C. Quiet conditions.
D. A mock-up of an actual blackjack table.

Answer: The rules used during the practice sessions should coincide with the actual rules you will encounter at the casino. In other words, use the most realistic conditions possible.

3. A card counter may be successful, assuming he or she ———.

A. Knows the right people at the casino.
B. Has a large enough bankroll.
C. Uses proper play strategy.
D. Slips the dealer a hundred.

Answer: With enough cash and the right conditions, a counter can be successful. It takes a huge bankroll, and perhaps a dealer "asleep at the wheel," to enable a counter to gain a very slight advantage over the house. Most of the time, an alert dealer will be "on" to large betting spreads and will stop the counter in his or her tracks!

4. *Progression Blackjack*'s argument with the card counting systems taught is with ———.

A. The betting and money management strategies.
B. The double-down strategies.
C. Insurance strategies.
D. All of the above.

Answer: I have no argument with the majority of the play strategies taught. I contend that the betting and money management systems are unrealistic and do not hold up under today's game. The average blackjack player cannot possibly afford the bankrolls these systems require.

5. Blackjack was low on the popularity scales in the 1930s because ———.

A. It was considered a sissy's game.
B. It was too difficult to learn.

C. Players were required to hit first.
D. The dealers were unfriendly.

Answer: The greatest advantage the dealer has over the player is that the player is required to hit first. This will never change and was the reason blackjack started out slow.

6. "Peeking" was a cheating technique used by dealers to determine the need to _____.

A. Deal a second.
B. Stand with current total.
C. Reshuffle.
D. None of the above.

Answer: Peeking the top card helped a dishonest dealer determine if dealing a second (the next card) was beneficial.

7. A casino would be very reluctant to mark a deck of cards because _____.

A. It is morally wrong.
B. It leaves physical evidence.
C. It is too expensive.
D. All of the above.

Answer: Casinos today make too much money honestly to risk cheating. Even the early casinos were reluctant to mark cards because it produced physical evidence that could be used to prosecute them.

8. The significance of the introduction of the multiple-deck shoe and the cut "indicator card" is/are _____.

A. End play was eliminated.
B. Several forms of cheating were eliminated.
C. The significance of the "count" was reduced.
D. All of the above.

Answer: The inventors of the multiple-deck shoe and indicator card were probably not aware of the total impact of such changes. End play was totally eliminated, cheating was made nearly impossible, and card counting was dealt a severe blow. This was undoubtedly the biggest change to the game of blackjack to date.

9. "Surrender" allows players to _____.

A. Pay half of the original bet to "throw in the towel," only if the dealer has an ace up.
B. Pay half of the original bet to "throw in the towel" after receipt of the first two cards.
C. Give up their seats at any time.
D. None of the above.

Answer: Surrender can be a money-saving option. It allows players to forfeit half of the wager to discontinue play upon receipt of their first two cards. It is a wise move when you have a 15 or 16 facing a 10-value card! Surrender was popular years ago but was eliminated because it was to the player's advantage. Some casinos are re-introducing the option today in order to attract players.

10. Proper play strategy is derived from _____.

A. Computer studies.
B. Intuition.
C. Experience.
D. All of the above.

Answer: Mathematicians and computers are responsible for the play strategies we learn today.

11. More liberal blackjack rules exist in Nevada than Atlantic City because _____.

A. Nevada has more money.
B. Nevada has more casinos.

C. Atlantic City gambling is more strictly governed by the state, which opposes rule variations.

D. The question is bogus, Atlantic City has more liberal rules than those found in Nevada.

Answer: Currently, Atlantic City gambling is very tightly controlled by the state. Efforts are being made to loosen these controls and to allow the casinos to be more competitive with Nevada. The day will have to come or Atlantic City is in for a rough ride!

12. Who benefits by keeping the card counting myth alive!

A. The casinos.
B. Card counting system authors.
C. A and B.
D. None of the above.

Answer: The question sounds like a line from the movie *JFK*! Of course the casinos and card counting authors benefit! Keep the myth alive, more books and videos will be sold and more suckers will flock to the casinos. It's a win-win situation for everyone but us little people! We are supposed to believe the card counting myth and risk our savings looking for that pot of gold.

13. Gambling package "front money" refers to _____.

A. The cost of meals and lodging.
B. The total price of a gambling junket.
C. Your total gambling bankroll less travel expenses.
D. The required amount of chips you must purchase to qualify for the package.

Answer: You are usually required to prove you have the required front money prior to boarding the plane or bus. Upon arrival at the casino you are required to purchase chips with that money. Packages that require front money are usually the best deals that can be found. Don't pass up a super deal because front money is involved. There is no requirement that you lose or even gamble with all those chips! The casinos are betting that you will gamble away all that money. Just risk what you can afford and cash in the rest. Better yet, win!

14. *Progression Blackjack* will come under attack because _____.

A. It exposes the card counting myth.
B. Casinos fear a progression bettor on a roll.
C. It isn't too kind to Atlantic City.
D. All of the above.

Answer: I am proud of A and B, but feel bad that I had to come down to hard on Atlantic City. I just hope conditions can improve there and it can once again be the great tourist attraction it used to be.

15. The game of blackjack should be _____.

A. Simple.
B. Exciting and fun.
C. Profitable.
D. All of the above.

Answer: I sincerely hope that by studying my book, blackjack will always be "all of the above" for you!

11

A Final Word

On a recent trip to Las Vegas I discovered that the competition for the "blackjack dollar" has heated up considerably since I first began writing *Progression Blackjack*. As predicted, the return to more liberal rules in favor of the player has begun! For this reason, I am providing an update on the blackjack conditions you will most likely encounter in Nevada at this time.

I am more excited than ever about our chances to walk away winners from the blackjack tables. An exhaustive search is no longer required to find casinos offering liberal rules. At least, not in Las Vegas! From the plushest hotels on the Strip to the smallest casinos downtown, one is currently able to find the "right table."

Many of the dealers at the Las Vegas Excaliber Hotel and Casino credit their owners with the Strip's return to the rules offering better chances for the players. They related to me that, upon opening, the Excaliber offered the player the ability to double-down on any two cards and also required the house to stand on a soft 17. This, they say, broke the ice and was the catalyst for others to follow suit. Whether or not this chain of events is accurate makes little difference. What does matter is that the rules have shifted in the right direction! Currently, most Vegas casinos offer double-down on any two cards. Some require the house to stand on soft 17 and others still stand on a hard 17. By all means, play at the house that requires the dealer to stand on soft 17 (assuming other rules being equal).

I'm happy to report that the number of double-deck games available has increased. In the double-deck games the player's cards are being dealt face down and the player is once again allowed to touch his or her cards. This aspect makes the players feel more involved and attracts more players. The cutting procedure is similar to that of the multiple-deck shoe and is designed to thwart card counting and end play. The popularity of the double-deck game has apparently overridden any fear the casino may have of players marking the cards. I don't profess any mathematical advantage of the double-deck game over the shoe. I sometimes prefer the ability to handle the cards as a change of pace. As with the single-deck games, to signal a hit the player scrapes the cards on the table. To stand, the player slides the cards under the original bet. To indicate a bust, the player simply lays the cards face up on the table in front of the wager. The same procedure is used to indicate a blackjack! To split, lay the cards face up, side by side in front of the wager. The split bet is placed behind the cards alongside the original bet. To double-down, lay the cards face up in front of the wager. The double-down bet is placed behind the original bet. To be safe, one should verbally inform the dealer of one's intentions. The dealer could mistake your desire to double-down on a pair of 5's for a split. That would be a bummer. To add a little spice and excitement to our lives, the casinos will generally deal all double-down cards face down. Those of you with weak tickers may sneak a peek; otherwise, you won't know the good news until after dealer's last play. It sure is nice when the dealer busts and the value of the double-down card makes no difference.

The number of single-deck games available continues to be small but the game can be found in most Las Vegas casinos. Once again, the players' cards are dealt face down, allowing more physical involvement. The drawback is, single-deck rules are less favorable for the player. Typically, the player is only allowed to double-down on a 9, 10 or 11. The player is also not allowed to double-down after a split. These subtle but significant changes kept my money off the single-deck tables!

The casinos continue to look for ways to speed up the game and get more money on the table. I was pleased to see that almost every house in Las Vegas has the dealer look in the "hole" when the ace is the dealer's up card. They had gotten away from this, as I mentioned earlier in the book. Of course, the dealer waits until all players have had a chance to take insurance, prior to peeking. Now, if the dealer has the natural, play is terminated and we don't have to go through all that agony. This speeds up play and eliminates the confusion of returning double-down and split wagers. It also returns us to the days of the "second look" when the old 4-spot is in the hole. As indicated, I am happy with this procedural change but would become concerned if the dealers peeked at any other time.

Some casinos are offering a new side bet in a game called Royal Match. The blackjack play is the same but the player is allowed to make a side wager of $1 to $100 on the possibility of receiving a flush on the first two cards. If the players' first two cards are of the same suit, the player received a 3-to-1 payoff on the side bet. If the two cards received happen to be a king and queen of the same suit, the player received a whopping 10-to-1 payoff on the side bet. Save your money and stick with the standard game. Royal Match is one of many blackjack variations that have come and gone through the years. I think this one will go faster than it came. There can't be that many suckers, can there!

While playing at the Excaliber I ran into a new version of blackjack that might just stick around for awhile. The game had just been introduced and the dealers were having a tough time dealing it. The game was tentatively called Triple Chance Blackjack. Essentially, the player receives one hand but plays it against three separate dealer's hands. Stay with me—this one gets complicated enough when you're there, let alone on paper! Every player has three stars in front of them, each representing a separate wager. Each star is color-coded to correspond with each of three dealer's star (each representing a separate hand). By placing a wager on all three stars, the player is betting against all three of the dealer's hands individually. The dealer gives all players one card up, and deals a down card on each of the dealer's stars. The dealer then deals each player a second card up and a down card on each of the dealer's three stars. The player now has one hand that competes separately with each of the dealer's three hands. The player's decision to hit, stand, double, or split is the same as with the standard blackjack game. The dealer must hit each of his or her hands until a soft 17 or

A FINAL WORD

greater is reached. The rub is, if the player busts, he or she immediately loses all three wagers. As you might have guessed, all standard play strategy is thrown out the window. Let's say you receive a two-card total of 14 and the dealer has a 4, 7 and 10 showing. What do you do? If you hit and bust, you lose it all. If you stand, the dealer may or may not bust on one or more of the hands. Say you have $10 bet on the red, white, and blue stars. You receive an 18. On the red hand the dealer draws to a 19. On the white hand the dealer busts. On the blue hand the dealer reaches 18. How do you fare? You lose the red, win the white, and push on the blue. The overall play resulted in a push. If you are lucky and receive standing hands you can clean up very quickly. If your cards are weak, you will lose very quickly. The game is very exciting and addictive. With the exception of playing one hand against three, the game plays very similar to normal blackjack. On a double-down you may double against one, two, or all three of the dealer's hands. In other words, let's say you receive a two-card total of 10. The dealer has a 6 up on the red hand, 8 up on the white hand, and a 10 up on the blue hand. You are allowed to double against any or all of the dealer's hands. Successful double-downs and splits can really bring home the bacon! When you receive a natural you get paid 3/2 on each and every one of the three wagers (unless one of the dealer's hands is a blackjack). When the dealer has an ace up you may take insurance on the corresponding star (hand), if desired. As mentioned earlier, basic play strategy does not apply. It appears that the best strategy is to not risk busting. This strategy relies on the dealer breaking on at least one of the three hands. I have not studied the game in enough detail to advocate a specific strategy. It's very difficult to stand on a 12 when the dealer has standing cards showing. On the other hand, it sure sucks when you receive a 10, and lose all three hands at once. Overall, I do not consider Triple Chance a true game of blackjack. I am discussing it because the game is likely to catch on, and will probably be with us for awhile. I want you to have a feel for what you're getting into before you sit down and play. If you decide to try Triple Chance, use the positive progression and hope that the high cards flow in your direction. Personally, I view this game as a crap-shoot. Give it a shot but run for cover if you are having bad luck.

The Triple Chance Blackjack game described is unique to the Circus Circus organization which owns the Excaliber. Credit for the origin of the idea must go to the Four Queens Casino. They developed the original version of the Triple Threat game. In the Four Queens version, the dealer only receives one up card which is played as part of all three dealer's hands. The Four Queens version is patented and royalties must be paid for the use. Thus, a slightly different version was developed by Circus Circus and most likely other casinos will follow.

My first encounter with Triple Chance Blackjack was quite interesting. I tried to use basic strategy but to no avail. Those more familiar with the game wasted no time telling me to quit taking hits. I had actually stumbled onto the table at a very good time. The majority of us were receiving good cards and were taking the house's money. I started playing $5 on each color ($15/hand) and had progressed to $25 ($75/hand). We were all winning, cheering and having a good old time. I was a few hundred dollars ahead and a couple of guys to my left were doing as well. My sister-in-law, Erin, lives in Vegas and had just arrived at the casino to visit and have dinner. My wife, Robin, and Erin stood behind me and cheered me on. It was getting on past diner time. Being a dedicated husband and great brother-in-law, I did not hesitate to leave a "hot" table. All right, I must admit that it took the two of them pulling on each arm to drag me away. After dinner I returned to the table. The piles of chips the players had won were all but gone. I was berated for leaving and having changed the luck. Obviously, I was back and we would now all start winning again. A very strange thing happened. We lost! My profit disappeared faster than I like to remember. Losing three bets at a shot can weigh heavily on the pocketbook. Although I departed the game slightly ahead, I felt defeated and the experience brought back unpleasant memories of my card counting days. I never returned to the Triple Chance tables that evening to play but did stop by on occasion to see how the players were doing. I never observed anyone having much luck. As you might have guessed, the rest of my gambling time was spent at the *real* tables. Where men are men and the blackjack is blackjack.

The low cost of a gambling junket continues to be the best deal going. With only a few days' notice my travel agent was able to offer me a four-night stay at the Hacienda for $120 or four-night stay at the Excaliber for $200. Each trip included airfare (from Dallas to Vegas), lodging, meals, shows and other perks. I opted for the

Excaliber package since I had never stayed there before. Everything was outstanding. The only complaint I have is that I had to arrange my own transportation from the airport to the hotel. That turned out to be no big deal because numerous rides are readily available. The food in Las Vegas continues to be fantastic and unbelievable low-priced, if and when you ever have to pay for it. In addition to a coupon book I received, I was able to get free meals by logging my playing time at the tables. To take advantage of this perk simply inform the pit boss that you want to be "rated." The food at the Excaliber was very good; however, I could not believe the outstanding spread that the Golden Nugget provided at their buffet. I must have eaten 25 crab claws, and that was just at the salad bar.

While at the tables I had many interesting conversations with the dealers concerning professional card counters. The feeling was that they probably exist but were somewhat like ghosts. One dealer explained that she once encountered a counter so good that he always made the correct play and won every hand. It sure sounded to me like more luck than skill. Counting has little to do with the cards you receive. What even intrigued me more was that she went on to explain that he was so good that he was able to always make the same bet. This is not what a counter would do! This particular dealer was extremely nice and fun to talk to. I was not about to jeopardize our good conversation by arguing with her. She was informative in many ways. She pointed me toward the royal match game and assisted the pit boss in explaining the evolution of the Triple Chance game.

As of this writing, the most liberal blackjack rules in Las Vegas can be found downtown at the Las Vegas Club. They justifiably claim the most liberal rules in the world. They offer double-down on any two or three cards, multiple ace splitting, surrender, no limitation on pair splitting (except aces), double-downs on splits, and automatic winner if dealt six cards totaling 21 or less. No other casino comes close to such liberal rules. It was the only casino I have ever encountered that allows a player to double-down after receipt of three cards! Robin and I were able to take avantage of these rules and significantly cut into the house's profits, much to the dismay of the management. The Las Vegas Club is far from plush, but offers the best opportunity to line your pockets with gold!

Dealers are required to hit to hard 17, which is only a minor concession considering the numerous other advantages. Relatively few poeple played blackjack at the Las Vegas Club, and those that did failed to utilize the liberal rules. This reinforced my belief that most players are blackjack illiterate!

Not all blackjack news is good. The players seem to be dumber than ever. Picture this: dealer has a 6 up, player doubles-down on 12 and busts. I almost went into cardiac arrest. This wasn't only stupid, it was suicide! I saw plays like this over and over again. Splitting face cards is commonplace. Busting against dealer's stiffs is in fashion. I never saw so many bonehead plays in my life. Several people hit soft twenties. At a double-deck table one guy hit a blackjack! He didn't double-down, he just took a hit. He wound up with a hard 21. When his original two cards were turned over I felt the dealer was waiting for the Candid Camera crew to emerge. Many of the worst players were unable to speak or understand English. Several people including dealers tried to get them to quit hitting bust hands against dealer's stiffs. They would nod their heads as if to understand and continue on as before. I never saw so much money thrown away in my life.

The only other bad news I can relate is that shuffle machines are in existence. I saw a couple of them being used at the Golden Nugget. I'm not sure how widespread they are or what their future will be. My hope is that I never see another one. I'm just glad that I spotted the machines after my meal and not before!

The improvements to the game that I encountered in Las Vegas can be found throughout Nevada and must eventually reach Atlantic City. The economy coupled with competition is making the gaming world better every day. Lower minimum table limits are becoming a necessity to compete for the recreational player's dollars. Even some cruise ships have recently opened tables under $5. Call those travel agents. When you arrive at the table, and win, tell them that Dahl sent you. If you happen to lose, tell them you're a counter!

Appendix A

Progression Craps

The "Winning Progression" taught in Chapter 4 need not be limited to blackjack. The strategy of positive progression is essential to winning at most games of chance. Only an idiot can argue with the theory behind making more money while winning than lost while losing. In addition to blackjack, I have successfully used progression betting at the craps tables.

Craps is, beyond a doubt, the most exciting of all casino games. Fortunes can be won or lost in just a few hours at the tables. It is also the only casino game that gives exact "odds" for a given bet, which I will discuss later. For these reasons, I could not conclude this book without a discussion of the game of craps.

A detailed study of craps is an entire book by itself. My intention here is to acquaint you with the game and to give you enough ammunition to hold your own at the tables. For the time being you will have to take my word for it when I tell you what bets to avoid. To augment the information that I present, you should seek other material, or wait for my next book!

The game of craps moves rapidly and cannot be easily understood by casual observation. For this reason, many prospective players feel intimidated and move on to the slots or the roulette wheel—an unwise decision. With a basic understanding of the game you will find it to be actually quite simple. As with blackjack, the knowledgeable craps player has a very good chance of success.

The Game of Craps

The object of the game of craps is to win money by betting on the outcome of the roll of two dice. The players wager that the "shooter" will either "pass" or "crap out." Other bets are available and will be discussed.

To proceed, I must define and discuss the following terms:

Shooter

The shooter, or roller, is the person rolling the dice. The shooter must make a wager prior to his or her first roll. The shooter wins if a 7 or 11 is thrown on the first roll of the dice and loses if a 2, 3 or 12 is thrown. When a 4, 5, 6, 8, 9 or 10 is thrown on the first roll, the shooter continues until the number is repeated or until a 7 is rolled. If the "point" is made, the shooter wins. If the 7 is rolled prior to the point, the shooter loses. The shooter maintains control of the dice until a point is established and lost (by throwing the 7). The dice are then passed to a player to the shooter's left. A player may decline to roll the dice; it is not necessary to be a shooter to play craps.

Pass/Pass Line

Pass is the term associated with "making the point." All players who bet that the shooter will win, place their bets on the pass line prior to the first roll of the dice. The pass bettors are winners if the first roll is a 7/11 or if the shooter makes the point. The pass line bets are lost if a 2, 3 or 12 is thrown on the first roll or if the shooter fails to make the point before a 7 is rolled. The shooter must have a bet on the pass line prior to the first roll. Players are not required to bet on the pass line. The pass line bets remain on the pass line in front of the player/shooter. The established point is indicated by a "puck" placed on the associated number. When the pass line bet is won, the winnings are placed beside the original bet. It is up to the player to remove all or part of the winnings before the next roll of the dice, otherwise the bet "rides."

Coming Out/Come Line

Coming out (come-out) is the term used to define the shooter's first roll of the dice. On the first roll the shooter may either win with a 7/11, lose with a 2/3/12, or establish a point (4/5/6/8/9/10).

After a point is established the shooter and players may place bets on the "come line" (come box). These wagers are treated as if they are new pass line bets. In other words, the next roll of the dice is considered the coming out roll for the bets on the come line. The purpose of the come bet is to allow the players and shooter to make bets on every roll of the dice.

Let's assume that the shooter's pass line point is 5. The outcome of the pass line bets will not be determined until a 5 is rolled again, or until a 7 is rolled. In the meantime, the shooter may roll several numbers that have no bearing on the pass line "decision." The come bet essentially serves as a new pass line bet for each roll of the dice. If a 6 was the first number rolled after making the come bet, it becomes the next point for those wagering on the come line. In this example, those with a bet on the pass line win if a 5 is rolled and those who have bet on the come win if a 6 is rolled. When a 7 is rolled with money on the come line, the come bet is won but all previous pass line and come line bets are lost. If an 11 is rolled, the come bet is won and all previous pass line and come bets are still "alive." If a 2, 3 or 12 is rolled, the come bet is lost and all previous pass line and come bets are, again, still alive.

After the "come bet" point is established, the come line wagers are moved from the come box to a square which identifies the point (labeled either 4, 5, 6, 8, 9 or 10). At this time, the next come bets may be made. When a come bet is won, the winnings and initial wager are placed in the come box in front of the bettor. Once again, the player must retrieve the money before the next roll of the dice or it will be considered a new come bet.

Through the use of the come bet, it is conceivable that a player could have bets on all of the possible points. All points rolled are winners! When the 7 shows, all pass line and come bets are lost except for the wagers currently on the come line.

Line Bet

The line bet (flat bet) is the wager made on the pass or come. Regardless of the point made, the payoff on a line bet is 1/1. If you wager $10 on the pass or come, you will receive $10 in winnings (if the bet is won).

Odds

The "odds" are based on the mathematical probability of a 7 being rolled before any given point. With two dice there are 36 possible combinations of 2-12. The frequencies of each total are as follows:

TOTAL	FREQUENCY OUT OF 36
2	1
3	2
4	3
5	4
6	5
7	6
8	5
9	4
10	3
11	2
12	1

As you can see from the chart, the odds of a 7 being rolled before a 4 are 6/36 to 3/36 which is 2/1. In other words, once a point is established, the odds are 2/1 against a 4 or 10, 3/2 against a 5 or 9, and 6/5 against a 6 or 8.

Taking the odds

Craps is the only game in which a player can receive a payoff based on the actual odds for a given event. In all other games the house pays the player less than the true odds. By paying a player less than the true odds, casinos make money! For example, in Chapter Two I discussed how the house pays 2/1 on a successful insurance bet when, in fact, the true odds are approximately 2.5/1. In the game of craps the odds against making the 4 are 2/1. By taking the odds you will actually receive 2/1 on your wager if the point is made!

It is essential to take the odds whenever possible. As mentioned earlier, line bets pay only 1/1, regardless of the point. This is a losing proposition without taking the odds.

Odds are taken on a given point after the point has been established. On the pass line, this is done by placing the odds wager behind the original line bet. On the come bets, this is done by handing the "dealer" the odds bet and telling him or her that you are taking the odds. Generally, odds are allowed up to the amount of the line bet. Most casinos will allow a player to take $5 odds on a $3 line bet if the point is 6 or 8 (6/5 odds). You must be careful to ensure that the wager made on the line is conducive to taking odds on all points. If the table does not deal in half dollars, ensure that odds taken on points 5 and 9 are in even-number increments, otherwise you will not receive the full 3/2 on the odds bet. If $5 were bet on the odds, the casino would only pay $7 in lieu of the $7.50 you should receive.

Assume we start with a $10 pass line bet. If the shooter rolls a 7 or 11 on the come out, we win $10. If a 2, 3 or 12 shows, we lose $10. Let's say the shooter rolls a 10, establishing the point. We should now take $10 in odds. If the shooter passes we will receive $10 for the original line bet and $20 (2/1) on the odds, for a total of $30.

Some casinos allow double odds. In this case, the player is allowed to make odds bets up to twice the initial line bet. By all means, take advantage of double odds every chance you have. Remember that the odds bet is the only "free" casino bet you will ever encounter. In fact, the odds is the only bet that the casinos never advertise. You won't hear a craps "dealer" tell you to take the odds. This is because they would rather you don't.

Wrong Betting

It is possible to bet against the shooter (with the house). This strategy is referred to as betting "wrong" (don't pass/don't come). To bet wrong, the player places the wager in the Don't Pass or Don't Come section of the table.

On the "come out," the wrong bettor loses if the shooter rolls a 7 or 11. To reduce the odds of a successful wrong bet, the casino "bars" either the 2 or 12. When a barred number is rolled on the come out, the wrong bettor neither wins nor loses. In other words, the barred number has no bearing on the decision. If the 2 is barred, the wrong bettor wins only if a 3 or 12 is rolled during the come out. If the 12 is barred, the player wins on the 2 or 3.

Once the point is established, the wrong bettors win if the 7 is rolled before the point. After the come out roll, the odds are in favor of the wrong bettor. The house is aware of this and allows the wrong bettors to pull all bets once the point is established. This is not the case with the pass and come bettors! Their bets may never be pulled once the point is determined.

Laying the Odds

As with the pass and come bettors, the "wrong" bettor is allowed to take odds on all line bets. In this case, however, the player must "lay" the odds. Since the odds of rolling a 7 are greater than making the point, the wrong bettor must put up more money than he or she would make. To lay odds on a 4 or 10 requires that the wrong bettor wager $20 to make $10 (if the shooter craps out). With the exception of having to lay the odds, the procedure is the same as for taking odds on both the pass and come bets.

Place Bets

Instead of having to bet on the pass line or come line, a player may simply place a bet on any of the possible points. He or she wins the bet if the number is rolled prior to the 7. The casinos usually advertise that place bets give true odds. This statement is simply not true. On a place bet the first $1 of every $5 bet is "flat" and the remaining $4 is with odds. If the point made was 9 you would receive 3/2 odds on the $4 and 1/1 odds on the $1 for a total of $7. This is how the house maintains an advantage on place bets.

Some gamblers take place bets on every point, wagering that the shooter will roll several numbers prior to a 7. The advantage of the place bet is that the player does not have to wait for a point to be rolled prior to betting on it. The disadvantage is that the wager does not receive true odds. Don't pass or don't come place bets are not allowed. You may only place bets that a point will be made.

Buy Bets

Buy bets are very similar to place bets. The major difference is that the player pays the house a fee up front and receives the correct odds on the total wager. The fee is usually 5% of the wager, but may vary if the house has a minimum buy bet. For example, the table may require a minimum fee of $1 for all buy bets. If the buy bet is $20, the cost is 5%. If the bet is less than $20, the percentage is greater. You may purchase "don't" buy bets and receive the actual odds on the bet. Ten dollars wagered on the 4 or 10 returns $5, for example.

Depending on the price of the buy bets and the size of the wagers, the advantage of buy bets over place bets is a toss-up. The player will have to decided which is more profitable on a case-by-case basis. The decision would be made as follows: Assume that the house table has a $1 buy bet minimum and you want to wager $20 on the 4. On the place bet, one of every $5 is flat, so you would make 1/1 on 4 of the dollars and 2/1 on the other 16, for a total of $36 (if the point is made). On the buy bet, $1 goes to the house off the top. You will receive 2/2 on the remaining $19 bet, for a total of $38. In this example the buy bet was obviously the better way to go!

Other Bets

If you have ever played or watched the game of craps, you may have heard of single throw and hard way bets. You should forget that these bets even exist because every one of them is a sucker bet! The payoffs seem to be high, but in reality are way out of line with the actual odds of such an event occurring. As stated earlier, you will have to take my word for it.

Play Strategy

I recommend playing strictly the pass and come line bets in conjunction with taking the maximum allowed odds at all times. This is the only play strategy that gives "free odds." To be successful, the player must increase the bet while winning and bet the minimum while losing. Using this strategy a player can easily build a $500 bankroll into thousands of dollars with a run of hot dice.

The reason I prefer the pass and come lines over the place and buy bets is that there is a good chance of winning with a 7 or 11 on the coming out roll. In fact, the odds of a 7 or 11 are 8/36 as compared to a craps (2, 3, or 12), which is 4/36. In other words, the chance of a successful pass on the first roll of the dice is twice that of a craps! The place and buy bets are only winners if the chosen point is rolled. In addition, the place and buy bet "odds" cost money, as previously explained.

Though the "wrong" bettor has the normal run of the dice on his or her side, I still prefer the pass and come. On the coming out roll the Don't Pass bettor has a 8/36 chance of losing and only a 3/36 (2 or 12 barred) chance of winning. After the point is established, the wrong bettor must lay odds to increase the chance of profits. It has always gone against the grain for me to risk more than I can win. I can't see risking $20 for a chance to win $10!

Craps Betting Progressions

The betting progressions found in table 4.1 work fine for craps. The $2 progression should be avoided if unable to take $5 odds on the 6 and 8. When the progression requires an odd number bet, be sure to make an even-number odds wager on the 5 and 9. The jump/skip bet rules do not apply in craps.

Playing Pass and Come

To select the craps table that is "right" for you, the following steps should be taken:

1. Seek out a casino that offers double odds. If none exist, single odds are fine.
2. Determine the betting progression to use based on your bankroll.
3. Ensure that the table minimum and maximum limits coincide with the chosen progression.
4. Look for a table where the dice are running "warm to hot." Do

not play if the shooters are regularly crapping out. Hot tables can easily be identified by the reactions of the players. You can hear the cheers and feel the winning frenzy when a shooter is on a "roll."

Once the table has been selected, it is time to play. For discussion purposes I will use the $10 progression with single odds. We will make the first bet on the pass line prior to the coming out roll.

Place a $10 bet on the pass line. If the shooter rolls a 7 or 11, make the second $10 bet. When the pass line bet is lost, return to the first bet of the progression. After the point is established, take $10 in odds.

Prior to the next roll, place a $10 bet on the come line. As with the pass line bet, take $10 odds when the point is established. The come line bets should be handled as a completely separate progression, independent of the pass line bet. The beginner should take the pass line bet and only one come bet. Have patience and wait for a decision. If the pass line bet is won, go to the next level of the progression. If the come bet is won, make another come bet at the next progression level. This strategy requires the player to only have to worry about two points at a time.

Make sure you are familiar with all table policies. On many tables the "odds" are "off" when a player is coming out. This means that when the pass line point is made, odds on the previous come bets do not apply on the next (coming out) roll. If a come point is rolled, the line wagers are paid and the odds are returned to the players. If the 7 is rolled, all come bets are lost and the odds are once again returned. Players may request that their odds "stay on" during the come out. Most casinos will oblige with this request.

Once familiar with the game, the player may make more than one come bet. I recommend that the average player never have more than four bets riding at one time. Be satisfied with the pass line bet and three come bets. It is very easy to lose track of your bets if not careful.

Practicing at Home

Craps is an extremely fast and furious game. A great deal of attention is required to ensure that winnings are picked up, odds are taken, and that the correct bet is made. By practicing at home you can be much better prepared to do battle at the tables.

All you need are some dice, paper, coins/chips and something to serve as a puck. I often use a shallow box to serve as a craps table.

Draw a pass and come line on the paper or in a box. Draw a square for each point. As the pass line point is established, place the puck in the proper square to indicate the point. As come line points are established, move the come bets to the associated squares. Follow the play procedure as I have outlined and become familiar with the game.

Money Management

Craps can be very expensive due to the pace of the game. The high rollers win or lose thousands of dollars in a short period of time. You could easily see $200 disappear in a matter of minutes. On the other hand, a player can easily double a bankroll in a matter of minutes!

When the dice are running "cold," get out of the game fast! Set a loss limit for each session and stick to it rigidly. Keep in mind that your minimum bet is the total of the line bet plus the odds. If on a $5 table with double odds, you will be risking at least $15 per point.

TABLE A.1

RECOMMENDED CRAPS BANKROLLS

Minumum Bet	Single Odds Bankroll	Double Odds Bankroll
$2	$200	$300
$5	$500	$750
$10	$1,000	$1,500
$25	$2,500	$3,750
$50	$5,000	$7,500
$100	$10,000	$15,000

Summary

As indicated by the minimum bankroll requirements, the game of craps can be much more expensive than blackjack. I know of no other game that can make or lose money as fast. When the dice are hot, the money pours in!

Always be prepared to lose at the dice tables. You should enter the game believing there is a chance to win large sums of money, but a likelihood of losing a predetermined limit.

Craps is not a game of skill; anyone can throw a pair of dice. All you can do is make the best percentage bets and hope the dice go your way.

If on a limited budget, you should only risk your blackjack profits at the craps tables. I usually end up on the craps tables after a successful venture on the blackjack tables.

Give craps a chance and quit after losing a few bets. Try it again another day and you might just run into those "hot dice." The chance of making a fortune on the craps table sure beats the heck out of the lottery!

List of Tables

Glossary

ANCHOR

The playing position closest to the dealer's right at a blackjack table.

The anchor is the last player to be dealt his or her cards and is the last player to play. For this reason, the anchor position is always the preferred location for card counters. The anchor is able to see the maximum number of cards prior to making a play decision.

Many players feel that the anchor has the greatest influence on the outcome of a given hand. This stems from the fact that the play of the anchor directly influences the cards received by the dealer. Heaven help the anchor who hits to a 15 and takes the dealer's bust card when the dealer has a stiff card showing!

The anchor is also a popular position merely due to the fact that it is only one of two spots (first base and anchor) where a player is not crammed between two other players. With the exception of comfort, there is really no playing advantage to any seat at a blackjack table. For every time an anchor screws up to help the dealer, he or she will most likely screw up and hurt the dealer. The seat is also referred to as "third base."

BALDWIN, ROGER R.

One of four United States Army mathematicians credited with developing the first play-strategy calculations to significantly reduce the house advantage.

BANKING GAME

A gambling game where the gambling establishment, or one player, opposes all other players.

BANKROLL

A total sum of money a player is willing to risk on a given trip or vacation.

The bankroll should not include money to be used for any purpose other than gambling. Money used for food, lodging, entertainment and transportation must not be considered part of the bankroll.

The bankroll determines the highest minimum bet a player can afford to make. The minimum table limit and betting scheme must be based on the bankroll. The quickest route to the poorhouse is to exercise improper money management.

The total bankroll may be divided into daily bankrolls which may be further divided into session money. The minimum bet made during a session should be based on the session money and not the total bankroll.

Typical card counting systems require anywhere from $500 to $5,000 to play at a $5 minimum table. *Progression Blackjack* only requires $250!

BARRED NUMBER (CRAPS)

When the house designates either the 2 or 12 as a non-winner (a stand-off) to the Don't Pass and Don't Come bettors on the come out.

By doing so, the casino reduces the odds of a successful wrong bet.

BET

The player's wager.

The bet must be made prior to the first card being dealt. Once the first card is dealt, the player is not allowed to touch or change the bet. A player is allowed to increase the bet on a double-down or split situation, in which cases the increased wager is placed behind or alongside the original bet.

Chips purchased from the dealer or a teller are used to make the bets. Cash may be used in lieu of chips at the request of the player. To do so, the player simply lays the cash in the designated betting area and states "money plays." The dealer's acknowledgment of the cash bet puts the money into play.

BETTING INCREMENT

The size of the minimum bet.

The betting increment should be based on the players bankroll and must be at or above the table minimum.

In Progression Blackjack the betting increment is the first bet of a given betting progression. As one's bankroll increases the progression and minimum betting increment may increase.

Also referred to as "betting unit."

BLACKJACK

The most commonly used name for the game of Twenty-One. A blackjack is actually a two-card total of 21 consisting of an ace and a 10-value card.

A player receives 3/2 upon receipt of a blackjack unless the dealer also has one. A total of 21 during a double-down or on a split is not considered a blackjack.

The 3/2 payoff on a blackjack is considered by many to be the greatest advantage gained by the count systems. The strategy is based on the player and dealer receiving more blackjacks in a 10-rich deck. Since the player is paid 3/2 and the dealer is not, the player has the advantage. This so-called advantage is minimal and rarely applies under today's game, as discussed in *Progression Blackjack*. Relying on this advantage has taken a hefty bite from many a counter's bankroll.

In the early days of Twenty-One, some casinos paid the players an extra bonus for a hand consisting of an ace and a black jack. Hence, the term blackjack was born.

Also referred to as a "natural."

BRAUN, JULIAN H.

Mr. Braun is credited with developing the most widely followed blackjack play strategy to date.

BREAK/BUST

When the dealer's or player's (hard) hand exceeds a total value of 21.

A break by the player is an automatic loss. A bust by the dealer only pays the players who have not previously broken. Requiring the players to hit first gives the casino the overall advantage. On a one-to-one basis, using proper play strategy, this advantage is minimized.

Most commonly referred to as a "bust."

BREAK/BUST CARD

The card received which causes the dealer or player to bust.

BURN CARD

The top card of a deck or shoe which is placed face down in the discard pile after the shuffle and cut, prior to the first card dealt.

Most casinos allow a player to view the burned card upon request. It is not normal to burn more than one card but there is no rule against it.

BUY BETS (CRAPS)

Placing a wager on any or all of the possible points and receiving correct odds. A commission must be paid up front for each bet made (usually 5%).

A buy bet may be made for or against the point to be made (come/don't come, etc.). The buy bet and place bet are very similar. Some players prefer buy bets over pass line and come bets because the number need only appear once to win.

CANTEY, WILBUR E.

One of four United States Army mathematicians credited with developing the first play-strategy calculations to significantly reduce the house advantage.

CARD COUNTING

Determining the wager and play strategy based on cards seen, relative to cards remaining in the deck/shoe.

Card counting is a group of systems developed to give the player a mathematical advantage over the house. The basic strategy revolves around the theory that a deck/shoe richer in 10-value cards is advantageous to the player.

As discussed in the Systems chapter, the advantages of card counting have significantly declined through the years. Even though the casino's countermeasures have eliminated all likelihood of gaining a significant advantage, would-be counters continue to buy books and videos on the subject. The days of the ten-cents-per-gallon gas as well as card counting should be considered past history!

Also referred to as "card casing."

COME BET (CRAPS)

A bet made on the come line any time after the initial come out roll of the dice.

The come bet wager is treated as though it is a new pass line bet. The player wins if the first roll is a 7 or 11 or if the shooter makes the point. The bet is lost if a 2, 3 or 12 is thrown on the first roll, or if the shooter fails to make the point before a 7 is rolled.

COME LINE (CRAPS)

The area of the craps table where the come bet is placed.

Also referred to as the "come box."

COMING OUT (CRAPS)

The first roll of the dice.

On the come out, pass bettors win on a 7 or 11 and lose on a 2, 3 or 12. Don't Pass bettors win on a 3 and 2 or 12 (depending on which is barred) and lose on a 7 or 11. Any other number rolled is the established point.

Also referred to as the "come out."

COMPS

Gambler's term referring to complimentary gifts given to players by the "house."

Comps often include free meals and lodging. Comps are usually given to high rollers to entice them to restrict their gambling to the host casino.

COUNTER

One who uses a card counting system to determine bets and play strategy.

Also referred to (by me) as a "sucker."

CRAPS

Game of dice where the player bets on the outcome of the roll of two dice. More specifically, it is a score of 2, 3 or 12 with a pair of dice.

Craps is considered by many the fastest and most exciting of all casino games. It is the only casino game that gives the exact odds for a given bet. Due to the rapid pace encountered at a craps table, the player must be well versed in the rules and procedures prior to play.

CRAP OUT

To lose by throwing a 2, 3 or 12 on the first roll of the dice (pass and come bets) or by rolling a 7 before the point is made.

DEALER

Employee of the casino who deals the game of blackjack. Is also the person who collects and pays off bets in the game of craps.

The dealer is the house representative at the blackjack table. He or she ensures that all house rules are enforced. The dealer is required to play his or her hand according to a predetermined set of rules. The dealer is never required to make a play decision. All dealer play is dictated by the rules of the house.

DEALING BOX

Original name for the box from which the cards are dealt. More commonly referred to as the "shoe."

DEALING SECONDS

A form of cheating whereby the dealer peeks at the top card and deals the next card instead of the top card (assuming he or she does not want to receive the top card).

A second would be dealt if the top card were a potential bust card.

DECISION (CRAPS)

The roll of the dice that determines a win or loss for a given bet.

On the come out roll, a 2/3/7/11/12 determines a winner or loser, thus, a decision. After the come out, only a 7 or the point determines a winner or loser.

DON'T COME/PASS (CRAPS)

A bet that the dice will not come/pass.

The Don't Pass bettor receives 1/1 on the flat bet but must lay the odds if he or she wants to take odds. On the come out, the Don't Pass bettor loses if the shooter rolls a 7 or 11 and wins on a 3, 2 or 12 (depending on which is barred). After the come out, the Don't Pass bettor wins if a 7 is rolled and loses if the point is made.

Also referred to as a "wrong bettor."

DOUBLE-DOWN

Placing an additional wager up to the amount of the original on the first two cards of a hand. The player is then only allowed one hit.

The double-down is usually only allowed if the value of the first two cards equals 10 or 11. Casinos can be found that allow the players to double-down on any two cards. To be successful, players must take full advantage of double-down play strategy.

The double-down can often make the difference between a winning or losing session. Casinos with more liberal double-down rules should always be sought out.

DOUBLE-UP SYSTEM

Betting strategy to double the bet after each loss.

A player with a large enough bankroll would never lose if allowed to double after each loss. The problem is, casinos prevent the possibility by establishing table limits. The primary reason for maximum table limits is to defend against the double-up bettor. More commonly referred to as the "negative progression" or "Martingale" systems.

END PLAY

When a dealer used the entire deck of cards, the card counter was able to determine bets and play strategy with the knowledge of what specific cards remained near the end of the deck.

End play was the primary tool used by counters to make large profits. Most of the stories about the success of counting stems from end play. The casinos have eliminated end play by never dealing out more than three-fourths of the deck/shoe. Today's players are lucky if they see two-thirds of the cards.

FARO
Popular card game in the West during the nineteenth century.

Faro is often depicted played in gambling halls on television westerns. It was a popular game in the casinos of Nevada during the 1930s and 1940s. Faro was supplanted by craps and blackjack in popularity and eventually disappeared.

FIRST BASE
The playing position closest to the dealer's left at the blackjack table.

The player at first base is the first to be dealt to and is the first to play.

FIVE-COUNT SYSTEM
Betting and play strategy based on counting 5's.

Counting 5's was one of the first systems developed which gave the player a slight mathematical advantage over the house. As 5's were depleted from the deck the advantage shifted to the players. The system was abandoned with the introduction of the 10-count system.

FLAT BET (CRAPS)
A craps bet made at even money.

The player is only paid one-to-one on all flat bets. To receive correct odds the player must take or lay the odds. Place bets and buy bets are not considered flat bets, even though a portion of the place bet is flat.

Also referred to as a "line bet."

FREE ODDS (CRAPS)
Term associated with receiving the true odds when taking the odds on a pass or come line bet.

FRONT MONEY
Term used to describe the money a casino requires a player to bring in order to qualify for a free or minimal cost trip to the casino.

The casino normally provides transportation, lodging and other perks when front money is required.

GAMBLING
The voluntary risking of a sum of money on the outsome of a game or other event.

GOODMAN, MIKE
Former Las Vegas pit boss and author of *How to Win*.
Mr. Goodman was one of the first blackjack authors to go against the grain and speak out against the count systems. He advocated a progression betting system similar to that used in *Progression Blackjack*.

HARD DOUBLE-DOWN
Double-down on two cards, neither of which is an ace.
See "double-down."

HARD HAND
Any hand without an ace or a hand where all aces are counted as one.

HIT
To receive an additional card at the player's request.
The dealer must hit or stay based on specific rules. Generally, the dealer is always required to hit until his or her hand totals 17 or more. The player is allowed to stay on any total.

HOLE CARD
The dealer's unexposed down card.
The hole card is not exposed until after all players' hands have been played. Basic strategy always assume the hole card to be a 10-value card.

HOUSE RULES
Set of rules established by the casino for the players and dealer to follow.
House rules are fairly standard throughout the world. Some casinos in Nevada have more liberal rules to attract more players.

IDIOT
One who splits tens!

INDEX NUMBER

Term used by counters which represents the count value divided by the number of remaining cards.

The index number is used to determine the player's advantage at any given time. Bets and play strategy vary with the index number.

INSURANCE

The player bets that the dealer has a blackjack when the dealer's up card is an ace.

Insurance may only be taken when the dealer has an ace up. Players are allowed to bet up to half of their initial wager. If the dealer has the blackjack, the insurance bets are paid off at 2/1. The player's initial bets are lost unless they also have a blackjack, which results in a push. If the dealer does not have the blackjack, the insurance bets are lost and play continues.

JUMP BETS

Large bet increases made by the early card counters when the count was to their liking. Also referred to in *Progression Blackjack* as skipping one level of the betting progression following a blackjack and two levels following a successful double-down or split.

Casinos look for huge bet increases by counters and will often shuffle following such an increase. Recent count systems acknowledge this fact and encourage players to make smaller jumps to conceal their system. In today's multiple-deck games, count systems rarely if ever qualify for such a jump. Be careful not to confuse the count system jump with the progression system jump/skip bet.

JUNKET

A relatively short gambling trip.

The term junket is used to describe a gambling trip of 24 hours or less.

LAYING THE ODDS (CRAPS)

To take odds, the wrong bettor must wager more money than he or she could expect to win.

Since the odds of rolling a 7 are greater than making the point, the Don't Pass bettor must put up more than he or she would make.

To lay odds on a 5 or 9 requires that the wrong bettor wager $30 to make $20 (if the shooter craps out).

LINE BET (CRAPS)
The flat wager made on pass/don't pass and come/don't come lines.

Line bets are always paid off at 1/1. The player is allowed to take or lay odds on the line bet.

Also referred to as a flat bet.

MAISEL, HERBERT
One of four United States Army mathematicians credited with developing the first play-strategy calculations to significantly reduce the house advantage.

MARKING CARDS
A form of cheating used by the house and players in which the back sides of the playing cards are coded with distinguishing marks.

The marked cards were used by a dealer in conjunction with dealing seconds (it eliminates peeking). The marked cards were used by the player to determine what the dealer's hole card was and to determine what the top card of the remaining deck was. Casinos rarely marked cards because it provided physical evidence which could be used in court. Players are unable to mark cards in games where all player's cards are dealt face up. In fact, in most games players are no longer allowed to touch the cards for that reason.

MARTINGALE SYSTEM
Betting strategy to double the bet after each loss.
See "double-up system."

MATCHPLAY CHIPS
Chips or coupons usually given to a player as part of a gambling package.

Matchplay chips represent cash when used in conjunction with a bet at one of the tables. For example, a player can bet five dollars and can match the bet with a matchplay chip (or coupon) for a total of ten dollars. If the player wins the bet, he or she receives ten dollars from the casino.

McDermott, James P.
One of four United States Army mathematicians credited with developing the first play-strategy calculations to significantly reduce the house advantage.

Mechanic
A blackjack dealer proficient in cheating.
Mechanics were brought into the game to stop a winner or to beat a "high roller." These dealers were well versed in peeking, dealing seconds, and stacking the deck.

Money Management
Determining the minimum bet one can afford to make based on the bankroll available.
Money management is quite simple yet is one of the most misused strategies. Players continue to make larger bets than their bankroll will support! The quickest way to wind up broke is to ignore proper money management.

Natural
A two-card total of 21 consisting of an ace and a 10-value card. See "blackjack."

Negative Progression
Betting strategy to double the bet after each loss. See "double-up system."

Odds
The probability of winning a given bet. In the game of craps, "odds" refers to the additional wager a player may make in conjunction with his or her flat bet.

Odds On/Off (craps)
Term to describe if the odds are on or off the come/don't come bets during a coming out roll.

Pass (craps)
When the shooter makes the point or throws a 7 or 11 on the come out roll.

Pass Line (Craps)

Area of the craps table in front of the players where pass bets are made.

Peeking

A form of cheating by the dealer whereby the dealer peeks at the top card of the deck to determine whether or not to deal a second.

Perks

Term often used to describe the extra and usually minor benefits received by a player as part of a gambling package.

Perks would include such items as free meals, shows, matchplay chips, etc.

Pit Boss

Supervisor over several blackjack tables.

The pit boss looks over all the tables in his or her area, monitors players, watches for cheating, and settles most arguments. The pit boss will often assist the players in calling a waitress over to the table.

Place Bets (Craps)

Placing a wager on any or all of the possible points.

The place bet can be made for or against the point being made. Part of a place bet is considered flat and the remaining portion is at correct odds. The place bet is similar to the buy bet.

Play Strategy

A self-imposed set of rules designed to give the player the best odds for defeating the dealer.

Play strategy should include: hitting, standing, splitting, doubling down, and insurance. A good play strategy combined with proper money management and a positive betting progression is the key to winning!

Point (Craps)

The number established on the come out roll that the shooter must roll again (before a 7) in order to pass.

POINT COUNT SYSTEM

Count system most generally used which keeps track of all cards played by assigning them a value.

The strategy of the point count is to determine how 10-value-card-rich the remaining deck/shoe is (an improvement on the 10-count system). The richer the deck/shoe, the greater the player advantage. The point count system was a powerful strategy at one time but has taken a beating due to the casino's defensive measures discussed in *Progression Blackjack*.

PONTOON

Early Australian, English and American mispronunciation of the French word for twenty-one (*vingt-et-un*).

The name pontoon has survived through the years and is still used by some in lieu of twenty-one or blackjack.

POSITIVE PROGRESSION

Betting strategy based on betting more money while winning than is bet while losing.

The positive progression is the only strategy that ensures that more money is bet when the cards are running hot. It also ensures that the player is always betting the minimum when the cards are cold. The positive progression is also the only system that allows an average player to make large bets using only the money he or she has just won from the house.

PUCK (CRAPS)

Round marker used to identify the established point.

PUSH

When the blackjack dealer and player tie. No money is won or lost.

If you ever run across a casino rule that gives pushes to the house, run for the hills!

ROLLER (CRAPS)

The person rolling the dice.

More commonly referred to as the "shooter."

SCARNE, JOHN

Early blackjack expert credited with developing the first four-deck blackjack dealing box.

Mr. Scarne wrote several gambling books and claimed to be the first blackjack player to use the count system, first to get barred from Nevada casinos, and the person responsible for the many Nevada blackjack rule changes.

SESSION MONEY

All or part of the bankroll designated to be used during a round of play.

If you plan on staying at the tables for just one session, the entire bankroll would be considered your session money. On the other hand, if you plan on playing for a few days, the bankroll should be divided into daily bankrolls and possibly subdivided into daily session money. In all cases the minimum bet to be made must be based on the session money. This money management technique will ensure you do not lose your bankroll on the first day of a three-day gambling vacation.

SEVEN-AND-A-HALF

Very early Italian game somewhat similar to twenty-one.

The Italians claim that twenty-one evolved from this game. The consensus is that the game of twenty-one originated in France, contrary to Italian belief.

SHOE

The box from which the cards are dealt.
Also referred to as the "dealing box.

SHOOTER (CRAPS)

The person rolling the dice. Also referred to as the "roller."

SHUFFLE TRACKING

The system of tracking cards during the shuffle process.

There are individuals who believe that they can gain an advantage over the casino by knowing where the dealer has positioned the cards during the shuffle. Good luck!

SKIP BET

Skipping one level of the progression betting scheme after a blackjack and two levels following a successful double-down or split.

The player should not skip two levels if the money to be risked is more than he or she just received.

The skip bet was developed to enable players to advance up the progression ladder more rapidly. It should always be used to maximize the advantages of the progression.

Also referred to as "jump bet."

SMITH, BENJAMIN F.

The man credited by Dr. Edward O. Thorp as the first blackjack player to use a successful count system.

SOFT HAND

A hand containing an ace where the ace is counted as 11 (total must be 21 or less).

SOFT DOUBLE-DOWN

Doubling down when one of the two cards is an ace.

Most casinos do not allow soft doubling. If available, take advantage.

See "double-down."

SPLIT

Option to play each of two like cards as a separate hand. A separate bet equal to the original wager must be made.

The player plays each split card as a separate hand. He or she receives cards on one card until it is good, or busts. Today's rules only allow the player to receive one card on split aces.

As with the double-down, the option to split is a tool that must be used to defeat the dealer. It is slightly more complicated than other strategies and must be studied and practiced. Many novices incorrectly split every time they get a pair.

SPREAD

The difference between the minimum and maximum bet that a card counting system allows.

STACKING THE DECK

Method used by blackjack dealers to cheat by arranging cards (during the shuffle) in an order intended to put the players at a disadvantage.

The clumping of high or low cards is considered a disadvantage to the players.

STAND

The decision to not receive another card.

STANDING CARD

Term used when the dealer has a 7 or greater showing.

Play strategy assumes that the dealer most likely has a standing hand and will not have to take a hit.

STANDING HAND

Hand requiring the dealer to stand.

In most casinos the dealer is required to stay on a hard 17 or greater.

STIFF

A hand with a total of 12 through 16 in which a hit may result in a bust.

STIFF SHOWING

Term used when the dealer has a 2 through 6 showing.

Play strategy assumes that the dealer will have to take one or more hits and is likely to bust.

SUCKER BET

Any bet made where the payoff is out of line with the odds of such an event occurring.

SURRENDER

Rule in blackjack that allows a player to throw in the hand after receipt of the first two cards at a cost of half of the original wager.

Surrender can be very advantageous to players and is rarely offered in today's games. Surrender is not allowed if dealer receives a blackjack.

TEN-COUNT SYSTEM
Counting strategy based on counting 10's.
See "Point count system."

THIRD BASE
The playing position closest to the dealer's right at a blackjack table.
See "anchor."

THORP, DR. EDWARD O.
Author of *Beat the Dealer*. Considered to be the foremost authority on blackjack.
Dr. Thorp is credited with developing the first count system to shift the odds in favor of the player. He is also regarded as the man responsible for the Nevada blackjack rule changes which occurred in the early 1960's.

TRUE ODDS (CRAPS)
Receiving a payoff equal to the actual odds for a given event to take place.
The payoff at the craps table on an odds bet is the only place where the house pays true odds.

TWENTY-ONE
Original name for the game of blackjack.
See "blackjack."

UNIT BET
The size of the minimum bet.
See "betting increment."

VAN JOHN
Early Australian, English and American mispronunciation of the French word for twenty-one (*vingt-et-en*).
The name Van John has survived through the years and is still used by some in lieu of twenty-one or blackjack.

V<small>INGT-ET-UN</small>

The French word for twenty-one.

It is believed that the game of twenty-one originated in France about the year 1700.

W<small>AR</small> Z<small>ONE</small>

The first levels/bets of a progression betting system.

The weakest aspect of a positive progression betting system is surviving in the war zone. I designed my progression to minimize the losses in this zone. Thus, a more powerful system.

W<small>IN</small> G<small>OAL</small>

A money management term that defines when a player should pocket his or her winnings and quit.

The win goals that many authors advocate are unrealistic. A player should not be expected to quit gambling after winning only twenty dollars! A realistic win goal is to take home as much money as you can!

W<small>RONG</small> B<small>ETTOR</small>

One who bets that the dice will not come/pass.

See "Don't Come/Pass."

Bibliography

Adams, Harold B. *The Guide to Legal Gambling*. New York: Citadel Press, 1966.

Ainslie, Tom. *How to Gamble in a Casino*. New York: Morrow, 1979.

Anderson, Ian. *Turning the Tables on Las Vegas*. New York: Vanguard, 1976.

Archer, John. *The Archer Method of Winning at 21*. Chicago: Regnery, 1973.

Arnold, Peter. *The Book of Gambling*. London/New York: Hamlyn, 1974.

Barnhart, Russell T. *Casino Gambling; Why You Win, Why You Lose*. New York: Dutton, 1977.

Berger, A.J. and Bruning, Nancy. *Lady Luck's Companion: How to Play, How to Enjoy, How to Bet, How to Win*. New York: Harper & Row, 1979.

Braun, Julian H. *How to Play Winning Blackjack*. Chicago: Data House, 1980.

Canfield, Richard A. *Blackjack Your Way to Riches*. Secaucus, NJ: L. Stuart, 1977.

Collver, Donald L. *Scientific Blackjack & Complete Casino Guide*. New York: Arco, 1966.

Cooper, Carl and Humble, Lance. *The World's Greatest Blackjack Book*. Garden City, NY: Doubleday, 1980.

Frey, Richard. *According to Hoyle*. New York: Fawcett Crest, 1985.

Goodman, Mike. *How to Win*. Los Angeles: Holloway House, 1972.

Goren, Charles H. *Go With The Odds: A Guide to Successful Gambling*. New York: Macmillan, 1969.

Graham, Virginia L. and Tulcea C. *A Book on Casino Gambling*. New York: Van Nostrand Reinhold, 1976.

Griffin, Peter A. *The Theory of Blackjack*. Las Vegas: Gambler's Book Club Press, 1979.

Hargrave, Catherine P. *History of Playing Cards*. Boston: Houghton Mifflin, 1930.

Ita, Koko. *21 Counting Methods to Beat 21*. Las Vegas: Gambler's Book Club Press, 1976.

Lemmel, Maurice. *Gambling: Nevada Style*. Garden City, NY: Dolphin Books, 1966.

McQuaid, Clement. *Gamblers Digest*. Northfield, IL: Digest Books, 1971.

Nolan, Walter I. *The Facts of Blackjack*. New York: Casino Press, 1984.

Ortiz, Darwin. *Darwin Ortiz on Casino Gambling*. New York: Dodd, Mead, 1986.

_____. *Gambling Scams*. New York: Dodd, Mead, 1984.

Patrick, John. *Casino Survival Kit*. Short Hills, NJ: John Patrick Prod., 1990.

Patterson, Jerry L. *Blackjack: A Winner's Handbook*. New York: Perigee Books, 1982.

Patterson, Jerry L. and Olsen, Eddie, *Break the Dealer*. New York: Perigee Books, 1982.

Puzo, Mario. *Inside Las Vegas*. New York: Grosset & Dunlap, 1977.

Revere, Lawrence. *Playing Blackjack As a Business*. Secaucus, NJ: L. Stuart, 1969.

Riddle, Major A. *The Weekend Gambler's Handbook*. New York: Random House, 1963.

Roberts, Stanley. *The Beginners Guide to Winning Blackjack*. Secaucus, NJ: L. Stuart, 1984.

Rudolph, Lee *Blackjack Consensus*. Bel Air, MD: Gambler's Analysis Inc., 1989.

Scarne, John. *Scarne's Encyclopedia of Games*. New York: Harper & Row, 1973.

_____. *Scarne's Guide to Casino Gambling*. New York: Simon & Schuster, 1978.

Silberstang, Edwin. *How to Gamble and Win*. New York: Watts, 1979.

_____. *The Winner's Guide to Casino Gambling*. New York: Holt, Rinehart and Winston, 1980.

Spanier, David. *Easy Money: Inside the Gambler's Mind*. London: Secker & Warburg, 1987.

Snyder, Arnold. *Blackjack for Profit*. CA: RG Enterprises, 1981.

Thorp, Edward O. *Beat the Dealer*. New York: Vintage Books, 1966.

Tulcea, C. *A Book on Casino Blackjack*. New York: Van Nostrand Reinhold, 1982.

Uston, Ken and Rapoport, Roger. *The Big Player*. New York: Holt, Rinehart and Winston, 1977.

Uston, Ken. *Million Dollar Blackjack*. CA: SRS Enterprises, 1981.

Wilson, Allan N. *The Casino Gambler's Guide*. New York: Harper & Row, 1970.

Wykes, Alan. *The Complete Illustrated Guide to Gambling*. Garden City, NY: Doubleday, 1964.

Gambling Books Ordering Information

Ask for any of the books listed below at your bookstore. Or to order direct from the publisher, call 1-800-447-BOOK (MasterCard or Visa), or send a check or money order for the books purchased (plus $4.00 shipping and handling for the first book ordered and $1.00 for each additional book) to Carol Publishing Group, 120 Enterprise Avenue, Dept. 51396, Secaucus, NJ 07094.

Beating the Wheel: The System That's Won More Than $6 Million, From Las Vegas to Monte Carlo by Russell T. Barnhart
$12.95 paper   0-8184-0553-8   (CAN $17.95)

Beat the House: Sixteen Ways to Win at Blackjack, Craps, Roulette, Baccarat and Other Table Games by Frederick Lembeck
$12.95 paper   0-8065-1607-0   (CAN $17.95)

Blackjack Your Way to Riches by Richard Albert Canfield
$12.95 paper   0-8184-0498-1   (CAN $17.95)

The Body Language of Poker: Mike Caro's Book of Tells by Mike Caro
$18.95 paper   0-89746-100-2   (CAN $26.95)

The Cheapskate's Guide to Las Vegas: Hotels, Gambling, Food, Entertainment, and Much More by Connie Emerson
$9.95 paper   0-8065-1530-9   (CAN $13.95)

The Complete Book of Sports Betting: A New, No Nonsense Approach to Sports Betting by Jack Moore
$14.95 paper   0-8184-0579-1   (CAN $20.95)

Darwin Ortiz on Casino Gambling: The Complete Guide to Playing and Winning by Darwin Ortiz
$14.95 paper   0-8184-0525-2   (CAN $20.95)

For Winners Only: The Only Casino Gambling Guide You'll Ever Need by Peter J. Andrews
$18.95 paper   0-8065-1728-X   (CAN $26.95)

Gambling Scams: How They Work, How to Detect Them, How to Protect Yourself by Darwin Ortiz
$11.95 paper   0-8184-0529-5   (CAN $15.95)

Gambling Times Guide to Blackjack by Stanley Roberts
$12.95 paper   0-89746-015-4   (CAN $17.95)

Gambling Times Guide to Craps by N.B. Winkless
$9.95 paper   0-89746-013-8   (CAN $13.95)

How to be Treated Like a High Roller by Robert Renneisen
$8.95 paper   0-8184-0580-4   (CAN $12.95)

John Patrick's Advanced Blackjack
$19.95 paper   0-8184-0582-1   (CAN $27.95)

John Patrick's Advanced Craps
$18.95 paper   0-8184-0577-5   (CAN $26.95)

John Patrick's Blackjack
$14.95 paper   0-8184-0555-4   (CAN $19.95)

John Patrick's Craps
$14.95 paper   0-8184-0554-6   (CAN $20.95)

John Patrick's Roulette
$16.95 paper   0-8184-0587-2   (CAN $22.95)

John Patrick's Slots
$12.95 paper   0-8184-0574-0   (CAN $17.95)

Million Dollar Blackjack by Ken Uston
$16.95 paper   0-89746-068-5   (CAN $23.95)

New Poker Games by Mike Caro
$5.95 paper   0-89746-040-5   (CAN $7.95)

Playing Blackjack as a Business by Lawrence Revere
$15.95 paper   0-8184-0064-1   (CAN $21.95)

Progression Blackjack: Exposing the Cardcounting Myth by Donald Dahl
$11.95 paper   0-8065-1396-9   (CAN $16.95)

Win at Video Poker: The Guide to Beating the Poker Machines by Roger Fleming
$9.95 paper   0-8065-1605-4   (CAN $13.95)

Winning at Slot Machines by Jim Regan
$5.95 paper   0-8065-0973-2   (CAN $7.95)

Winning Blackjack in Atlantic City and Around the World by Thomas Gaffney
$7.95 paper   0-8065-1178-8   (CAN $10.95)

Winning Blackjack Without Counting Cards by David S. Popik
$9.95 paper   0-8065-0963-5   (CAN $13.95)

(Prices subject to change; books subject to availability)